Praise for *Visits from Heaven*

"I have known Dr. Pete Deison for many years now and have utmost respect for his wisdom and love of people. In *Visits from Heaven*, Deison's understanding and compassion shine throughout the book to help its readers work their way through the stages of grief, including from the loss of loved ones who have chosen suicide. He also encourages us with the hopes and wonders of what heaven will be like—for us as believers as well as for believers who may have committed suicide."

—Paul Meier, MD
Author and cofounder, Meier Clinics

"Nothing shatters the soul like the sudden death of a loved one. Life explodes into fiery fragments, and we stagger to make sense of it all. My courageous friend Pete Deison not only dares to bare his heartbreak but boldly storms the portals of heaven and scours God's Word to find answers. Like a seasoned fireman he guides his readers through choking debris into fresh air of understanding and exquisite hope. Here is a book perfectly suited for our distressing days."

—Jeanne Hendricks
Author; widow of Dr. Howard Hendricks

"Out of tragedy and heartache Pete Deison discovered hope that heals. Now in *Visits from Heaven* he offers that inspiring gift to us. I highly recommend it."

—Dr. Robert Lewis
Author and founder, Men's Fraternity

D0483393

"Shock, anguish, pain, emptiness, and horror are the emotions I initially felt in reading the saga of Harriet and Pete Deison. However, as I progressed I came to the realization that what is found here is a love story that was both broken by human frailty but also characterized by a love that could only find its origins in heaven. What I found was a work that did not dismiss the terror of human loss, the anguish of living, and the vacuous emptiness of loneliness, but offers deep insight and help for fellow travelers into the dark mire of pain and loss. The theocentric and bibliocentric lens through which Pete traverses the nadir of his soul is remarkable; the practical insight and balanced perceptions are wonderful. I cried when I read it, but I placed the volume in my library as a choice treasure of the experience of divine mercy in the midst of pained trust. Some of what is offered may seem controversial and the use of some passages questionable, but the great message of the book is that there is a world of reality that is far larger and more real than this one; there is hope to be found in the character of God that eternity and time interconnect though seemingly in a disjointed fashion, but actually not so much as we earthlings think; there is profound reason biblically and otherwise that our separations are only for a time, our pains having a purpose with reunions afterward that transcend time. 'But now faith, hope, love abide these three; but the greatest of these is love' (1 Cor. 13:13)."

—JOHN D. HANNAH
DISTINGUISHED PROFESSOR OF HISTORICAL THEOLOGY
RESEARCH PROFESSOR OF THEOLOGICAL STUDIES,
DALLAS THEOLOGICAL SEMINARY

"A book written with the tears of Christ, *Visits from Heaven* provides perspective, hope, and inspiration from the valley of the shadow of death. Pete Deison faced the most excruciating loss one can face as a husband. As a pastor, he had to relearn to care for his own soul; and as a writer he charts the map for the deepest terrains of his soul for our sakes. This book is a true gift to those of us walking through the darkness of our earthly path, and a rare treasure of heavenly vision."

—MAKOTO FUJIMURA
ARTIST AND DIRECTOR, BREHM CENTER

"Pete Deison has done an outstanding job of embracing his grief and aggressively seeking answers to difficult if not impossible questions. He teaches us some valuable lessons about how to grieve. I recommend his book to anyone who has experienced the loss of a loved one."

—SCOTT SUSONG
ASSISTANT PASTOR, SECOND BAPTIST CHURCH

"Pete Deison has written a book of excruciating honesty. The depth of disclosure of the issues of mental illness, deep love, suicide, and recovery is explored in an uncommon, almost page-turning way. Pete and his wife, Harriet, have been friends of ours for a long time. Her death rocked us to the core. Pete has been given uncommon grace in unpacking an extraordinary set of circumstances that would have shattered a lesser man. This is a breathtaking story for everyone but a timeless book for anyone who's been in the intimate orbit of mental illness."

—E. PEB JACKSON
PRESIDENT, JACKSON CONSULTING GROUP

"With compelling evidence, biblical precision, and astounding life-changing encounters, fellow struggler Pete Deison shows us how our tissue-thin connection to heaven—from earth—is easily penetrated by faith. Read and be delighted."

—DR. EMMETT COOPER
AUTHOR, THE HONEYWORD BIBLE
FOUNDER AND PRESIDENT, HONEYWORD YOU-NIVERSITY.

"You have wisdom no one wants. Wisdom honed through an experience no one would ever want to endure, but wisdom nonetheless. Thank you for addressing depression and suicide in a head-on, authentic, and vulnerable manner. Most people in the church are afraid to broach these topics. Thank you for not being one of those people."

—GREG MURTHA
FOUNDER, LIVING WITH A LIMP
CHIEF RELATIONSHIP OFFICER, IDONATE
FORMER PRESIDENT, HALFTIME

"The minute *Visits from Heaven* arrived in the mail, I opened it and read it, finishing it in just a few hours. I laughed and cried, and cried some more, loving the way it was based on Scripture. Pete's personal insights, and the beautiful picture portraying God's Truth, touched my heart. It is certainly a book I will refer to again and again. No doubt God will use his walk through grief to help others and draw them to Himself."

—JUDY SUSONG
LIFELONG FRIEND

"Pete Deison's *Visits from Heaven* is a frank, biblically connected discussion of love, suicide, grief, comfort, and heaven. It discusses things we wonder about with a combination of care and mystery. His trust in God and resting in His sovereignty comes through clearly in ways from which we can learn, even if there are things we cannot 'figure out.' Read it, ponder what it says, and renew your trust in our gracious God."

—DARRELL L. BOCK
EXECUTIVE DIRECTOR FOR CULTURAL ENGAGEMENT,
HOWARD G. HENDRICKS CENTER FOR CHRISTIAN
LEADERSHIP AND CULTURAL ENGAGEMENT
SENIOR RESEARCH PROFESSOR OF NEW TESTAMENT
STUDIES, DALLAS THEOLOGICAL SEMINARY

"Beautifully tracing his journey from grief to hope, Pete faithfully desires to seek out God's truth in the midst of his confusion and sorrow, striving to set the focus on Jesus, in both his own life and the lives of others. He sets an example of what it looks like to carefully listen for the voice of the Lord and trust Him in all circumstances. Full of encouragement and new insight, this book will be a blessing for those with questions about suicide, grief, heaven, and seeking the Lord's voice, all while focusing on the hope and peace we find in Christ alone, even in the midst of despair."

—KARA DAVIS
STUDENT, UNIVERSITY OF ARKANSAS

"I knew Harriet Deison in high school, and Pete at the University of Texas. I have felt deep sorrow for Pete in the loss of his beloved Harriet, but I have also rejoiced with him in his journey through grief into hope and trust in God and the goodness that is in heaven. In this book, Pete will challenge your thinking regarding the door between earth and heaven, the reality of God's voice in dreams, and the ways God speaks to and through us. I encourage you to join Pete on this journey."

—JUDY DOUGLASS
WRITER, SPEAKER, ENCOURAGER
OFFICE OF THE PRESIDENT, CRU
AUTHOR OF *LETTERS TO MY CHILDREN: SECRETS OF SUCCESS*

"Journey with Dr. Pete Deison, the mourner-learner (but ever the teacher), as he walks through the landscape of grief. Since none of us holds grief-exempt status, we can learn from his contagious vulnerability in the face of excruciating loss that we really are *unforsaken*. Sovereign purpose in permitting the harshness of premature death is softened by earth's close proximity to heaven. While he does not make normative claims from his precious hagiography, we are nevertheless convinced that there is a custom tailoring of all grievous circumstances for our good. Having watched Pete throughout the grief-recovery process from hell's attempted one-upmanship, I am so grateful my gifted seminary-mate wrote this book of honor and remembrance, but one of instruction and guidance too. May many a grief-weakened soul gain spiritual perspective and practical help during times of tears and fears through this authentic expression of grace in grief."

—RAMESH RICHARD, ThD, PhD
PRESIDENT, RAMESH RICHARD EVANGELISM
AND CHURCH HEALTH (RREACH)
PROFESSOR, GLOBAL THEOLOGICAL ENGAGEMENT AND
PASTORAL MINISTRIES, DALLAS THEOLOGICAL SEMINARY

"In a world where people are driven by social media to stay connected, Pete reveals his love story and the beautiful connection he had with his wife, Harriet, long after she arrived in heaven. Though we don't know much about the aspects of relationships in heaven, Pete shares hope in his own experiences and makes heaven seem so real. You will be brought to tears as you see God's hand at work and the peace He has given to Pete after such a devastating loss."

—KEITH CHANCEY, MACE
KANAKUK KAMPS
KANAKUK INSTITUTE

"Though an easy read, this book has significant theological depth. You will also find this book is one of the best on the subject of heaven. But on this side of eternity, you'll gain in-depth insights on some of life's greatest challenges, namely grief, depression, and suicide. I'm confident all readers will advance and have a greater understanding of some of the big mysteries of life—and death!"

—DR. GENE A. GETZ
PROFESSOR, PASTOR, AUTHOR

VISITS FROM HEAVEN

One Man's Eye-Opening Encounter with Death,
Grief, and Comfort from the Other Side

PETE DEISON

W PUBLISHING GROUP

AN IMPRINT OF THOMAS NELSON

Published in Nashville, Tennessee, by W Publishing, an imprint of Thomas Nelson.

Published in association with the literary agency of Wolgemuth & Associates, Inc.

Thomas Nelson titles may be purchased in bulk for educational, business, fundraising, or sales promotional use. For information, please e-mail SpecialMarkets@ ThomasNelson.com.

Any Internet addresses, phone numbers, or company or product information printed in this book are offered as a resource and are not intended in any way to be or to imply an endorsement by Thomas Nelson, nor does Thomas Nelson vouch for the existence, content, or services of these sites, phone numbers, companies, or products beyond the life of this book.

Some names and identifying details have been changed to protect the privacy of the individuals involved.

Unless otherwise noted, Scripture quotations are taken from New American Standard Bible®. Copyright © 1960, 1962, 1963, 1968, 1971, 1972, 1973, 1975, 1977, 1995 by The Lockman Foundation. Used by permission. (www.Lockman.org)

Scripture quotations marked THE MESSAGE are from *The Message*. Copyright © by Eugene H. Peterson 1993, 1994, 1995, 1996, 2000, 2001, 2002. Used by permission of Tyndale House Publishers, Inc.

Scripture quotations marked NIV are from the Holy Bible, New International Version®, NIV®. Copyright © 1973, 1978, 1984, 2011 by Biblica, Inc.® Used by permission of Zondervan. All rights reserved worldwide. www.zondervan.com. The "NIV" and "New International Version" are trademarks registered in the United States Patent and Trademark Office by Biblica, Inc.®

Italics in Scripture verses are the author's own emphasis.

ISBN 978-0-7180-8360-1 (SC)
ISBN 978-0-7180-8404-2 (eBook)

Library of Congress Cataloging-in-Publication Data

Library of Congress Control Number: 2016950612

Printed in the United States of America

16 17 18 19 20   RRD   10 9 8 7 6 5 4 3 2 1

Life is always an intertwining work of heaven and earth. You cannot have one without the other. Therefore, all dedications must begin with our Father, who gives us the good gifts. In addition, when that good gift comes down as a person like Harriet Schoellkopf Deison, I stand in awe at the magnitude of God's goodness. She wasn't perfect, yet she was the perfect gift for me, just as my Father in heaven intended. Thank you, Harriet, for blessing my life in more ways than I ever knew you could or would. Even now with you in heaven, the earthly benefits you gave me still bless my life. And thank You, good and Holy Father.

Every good thing given and every perfect gift is from above, coming down from the Father of lights, with whom there is no variation or shifting shadow.

—JAMES 1:17

CONTENTS

Contents

PART 1

A HEAVENLY
LOVE STORY

CHAPTER 1

IN THE BEGINNING

*If heaven is a world of love, then the way to heaven is the
way of love.*

—STEPHEN J. NICHOLS, *HEAVEN ON EARTH*

Head over heels in love is a literal memory I can't forget. After
only a few short weeks, I knew the woman I was dating was
the woman of my dreams. It was my junior year at the University
of Texas, and one day, walking up to the classroom building with
my head in the clouds, I started up the staircase but missed the top
step. I tripped, fell, tore my pants, and cut my leg. Trying to stand
on the steep bank, I tumbled down the hill, landing in the gutter.
I was still thinking about Harriet as the water in the gutter seeped
into my shirt and I heard the bell ring. Scrambling up the hill, I
ran into the classroom and everyone gasped. There I stood with
torn pants, mud and leaves everywhere. The first words out of my
mouth were, "I'm in love!" Everyone laughed and went right back
to talking. They all understood. Why? Love makes you do crazy
things.

When love seems divine, it captures you in a world of wonder. Everything changes. Everything feels different and fresh. The
feeling is hard to explain. Songwriters try, and poets embellish it;

everyone knows it when it happens. It feels like a bit of heaven. I have since learned that visits from heaven occur more regularly than we know. We just don't recognize their true origin.

Today as I look back on how I met Harriet, the heavenly source of our connection is as clear as crystal. I am amazed at how perfectly God was working behind the scenes to bring us together and fulfill our desires for love. God had been preparing us for that moment for many years.

❦

I was the seventh child born to my parents, arriving more than four years after my closest brother. My parents were strongly religious, loving, and willing to accept whatever God gave them—but another child was not on their wish list. My mother later admitted to me that when I was born, she said to God, "I don't need another child; this one is Yours. I just pray that he will go into the ministry." I may have been unintended, but I was not unloved. I was cherished and my needs were met.

With a highly religious mother and pastor father, I grew up with a strong God-consciousness. But when I was eleven, my family endured a trauma that unsettled me. We lived in the pine-forested logging area of East Texas, and my parents were driving home after picking up my sister from college. As they topped a hill on Highway 75 near Centerville, they suddenly faced a logging truck stalled in the road. My father slammed on the brakes and swerved to the right. But it was too late. The left side of the car crashed into the truck, killing my father. By God's grace, my mother and sister survived. My mother's recovery took months, and she bore scars until the day she died.

I struggled to absorb this tragedy and understand why it had happened. But I was just too young and immature to have any comprehension of God and His mysterious ways.

After graduating from high school, I enrolled at the University of Texas in Austin. During my first semester, I met someone who asked me about my faith. Sensing that I was uncertain about it, he helped me fit together the pieces about God and faith and the Bible I had collected over the years but had not yet connected. At that point, I realized God was seeking to have a personal relationship with me, and that changed the whole trajectory of my life. I finally understood my faith to be in a Person, not in an idea, and I came into a real relationship with God. With this new understanding of faith, my life took a different direction.

I had always wanted to marry a girl who was pretty and personable, but after I became a committed believer, I wanted a wife who would also be a partner in my new journey of faith. But I had no idea how to go about finding such a girl. For some reason, it never entered my immature mind to ask God to send me a life mate. As I floundered on my own, my first experiences in dating and courtship were disasters.

By the time I began my junior year at UT, I had already been through three relationships that ended in heartache and pain. At the young age of twenty, I realized I needed help. I was determined not to put another girl through the pain of rejection, and equally determined to avoid a repeat of it myself. So I gave up my search and decided to leave it up to God: "I don't want to date anymore. I want You to choose my lifelong mate and bring her to me."

Since I had put my marital future in God's hands, I decided I no longer needed free evenings for my social life, so I took a job that required me to work seven nights a week. Don't get me wrong:

I wasn't punishing myself for my relational failures. The job provided good pay and good discipline, both of which I sorely needed. Two years of goofing off at college taught me I might never get out if I didn't get serious. The job gave me considerable free time to study—and did I ever need that! I even had an office and a title, and a fairly impressive one, I thought. I was the assistant night sergeant at arms for the senate chamber of the Texas state legislature. My job was to prepare the night meeting rooms for the senators' committee meetings as needed. Most of the time I just sat at my desk, on call, and studied.

The Texas senate does not meet during Christmas break, which freed me to go on a trip to Chula Vista, Mexico, to restore an old mission. The following week the student campus ministry that supervised the trip had its weekly meeting, and I was asked to make a report on the trip.

A girl who came often to our campus ministry asked a Pi Phi sorority sister to accompany her to that meeting. The friend's name was Harriet Schoellkopf. When I met Harriet, I remember thinking she was exceptionally pretty, very nice, intelligent, and possibly a committed Christian—just the type of person our campus ministry ought to have in the student group. And I also thought she might be a great date. In other words, I saw her both as a project and a prospect. But such thoughts remained submerged in my subconscious. At that moment, I had a report to give.

Two weeks later, a coworker at the capitol offered to cover for me if I wanted to go to the next campus ministry meeting. I hadn't dated anyone in more than six months, but out of the blue the thought hit me that I should take a girl to the event. Since I had determined not to date until God pointed the way, I prayed and asked Him for guidance. Harriet came immediately to my mind. I got the number of the Pi Phi house and picked up the phone to dial it.

At that exact moment, I heard the voices of people coming into my office—a thing that seldom happened. I was on the second floor of the capitol in the senate wing. It wasn't a place anyone would accidentally run across, nor was it easy to find even if one was looking for it. I quickly replaced the phone receiver and turned around just as Harriet and her friend walked through the door. I stood there gaping like an idiot, speechless. I had just asked God whom I might take to the meeting, thought of Harriet, gotten her number, and started to dial—and right at that moment, there she was. Not merely a voice on the phone, but in the flesh. I know now that it was a visit from heaven. I don't mean Harriet was an angel, though ironically the Pi Phi nickname is "angels." But believe me, at that moment she looked heavenly.

I recovered my composure and greeted my two visitors. In response, Harriet's friend explained why they had come. "My dad is an attorney in an office across the street," she said. "I needed to see him and invited Harriet to come with me. Afterward we remembered that you worked here, so we just thought we'd drop by and say hi."

So the girls had dropped by as a spur-of-the-moment afterthought? Hardly! Later I learned they had devised this carefully laid plan just so Harriet could see me again. As I look back on that day, I see God's love at work. He had inspired Harriet to come by my office as part of His strategy to bring to me my future mate just as surely as He brought Eve to Adam.

When Harriet walked into my office that evening, I had no idea it would be a life-changing visit. Yet I was as surprised as

Adam and Eve were when they encountered God. Thank goodness I didn't hide, but I was speechless.

That is how heaven works now, because that is the way it was intended to be in the beginning. If we could only see just how connected heaven and earth are, we could see how many heavenly visits occur every day. In fact, this intimate connection between heaven and earth is the way the whole story begins—not just my story with Harriet but the big story of our lives. It is as plain as the words on a page: "In the beginning God created the heavens and the earth" (Genesis 1:1). Notice the order: heaven existed before earth. Then He created us, male and female, and gave the first couple an idyllic garden as their home. He personally demonstrated to them just how closely earth and heaven are connected and how natural and beautiful this connection is: "They heard the sound of the LORD God walking in the garden in the cool of the day" (Genesis 3:8).

God's first visit after setting everything in place was as if He simply stepped out of His back door and took a leisurely walk through His new creation, admiring His magnificent garden and anticipating a joyful conversation with these two new beings He made to bear His very own image. How natural! How normal! Visits from heaven were to be as commonplace to creation as if God were our next-door neighbor.

Why Harriet was so interested in seeing me that night is a story in itself. She was a religious girl and had been dating a young man who intended to follow his father's footsteps into the ministry. They had even begun to talk of marriage. But the fact that they were both Christians didn't mean they were on the same page spiritually.

As the relationship progressed, the differences in their faith became more and more apparent. These differences began to erode the relationship.

In the weeks before I met her, Harriet expressed to her boyfriend that she wanted to attend a few meetings of various campus ministries. He objected strongly to her getting involved with what he viewed as "extreme" organizations. Harriet resented his attempts to control her life and especially her faith and flatly told him that he was not going to tell her what to do. The conversation went downhill from there and ended with her calling off the relationship the night before I met her.

Harriet was still upset when her sorority sister asked her to attend a campus ministry meeting that same night. She jumped at the chance—probably mostly in defiance. But after hearing me speak that night, she went back to her room and wrote in her diary, "I think I've met the man I want to marry."

I believe it is true that marriage is made in heaven—that is, when two people are seeking God's plan. This is why I can say Harriet's visit to my office was in fact a heavenly visit. Neither of us was aware of it at the time, because we experienced the relationship that grew out of the meeting as natural infatuation that blossomed quickly into earthly love. We had a dim sense that our relationship was directed from above, but we had no conception of the extent to which God had been involved in it. Therefore, we had no way to acknowledge the depth of heaven's intimate and ongoing involvement in our courtship.

Harriet and I spent time together every day and quickly became immersed in each other's lives. We shared our pasts and delighted in our present experiences. She laughed at my jokes, and I endured her practical jokes, which persisted throughout our entire life together.

On one of our early dates, I took her to a fast-food restaurant for burgers. Before we placed our order, she decided she didn't want a burger—just a drink and an order of fries. I wanted the whole meal deal, so we placed our order and sat down. While we waited, I went to the restroom. When I came back, our food had arrived. My burger was wrapped—as they often used to be—with paper around the bottom half, leaving the top half exposed. I ate the top half, and as I removed the paper to begin chomping the rest, I discovered that a huge bite had been taken out of the bottom.

"The waitress must have done it," Harriet said with a straight face.

I knew better, of course, but I could never get her to confess.

Harriet shared my dreams of being involved with campus ministry. She even told me that for years her favorite movie had been *A Man Called Peter*, a film based on the life of Peter Marshall, a Scottish man who had a life-changing encounter with God and became a Presbyterian pastor and eventually the chaplain for the US Senate in Washington, DC. We didn't know it at the time, but I was her Peter, who would one day also become a Presbyterian pastor.

Though Harriet and I had not yet discussed marriage, it was clear to both of us that our relationship was heading in that direction. She broke the news to her parents that she had become seriously involved with me, and it appeared that marriage was possible in our future.

Harriet's father was a successful manufacturer of hunting clothing. Naturally, he and Harriet's mother wanted to meet the boy who was pursuing their daughter. Her father had scheduled a javelina hunting trip that happened to coincide with UT's spring break, so he asked Harriet to invite me to the event.

She issued the invitation, and while I was considering whether I could go, I got a call that stopped me in my tracks and threw me into uncertainty and confusion.

"Hello, Pete," said the sweet female voice on the phone. "Do you remember me? I'm Karen. We met last summer."

Karen! She was a student leader I had met who was not only passionate about ministry but was someone I was attracted to. *What in the world could she be calling about?* I pulled myself together and replied, "Yes, of course I remember. We had a great time at the conference. Did you and your fiancé get married?"

"No, we broke up. He didn't have the commitment I wanted in a man. And you have often been on my mind since. Spring break is coming up in a few weeks, and I was wondering if you might be able to come up to Wisconsin for a visit. We could spend some time together and get to know each other better."

The longer we talked, the more it became clear that she was seriously interested in pursuing a relationship. I mumbled something about getting back to her with an answer and finished the conversation as quickly as I could.

When I hung up, my palms were sweating. Why didn't I just say no to Karen? I was already in a delightful and growing relationship with a wonderful girl whom I was thinking seriously of marrying. Now I had a real dilemma on my hands. Two highly attractive, engaging Christian girls had invited me to spend spring break with them, and I had to make a wrenching decision.

After three broken relationships, I had recognized my inability to navigate the minefield of college dating and had put the whole mate-finding task in God's hands. It seemed clear to me that Harriet was His answer to my prayer, and I still sincerely hoped so. But "clear *to me*" didn't necessarily mean the relationship was from God. After all, we had only been together six weeks. Maybe I had fooled myself into thinking Harriet was the one. Maybe what I had with Harriet was mere infatuation, which blinded my reason. Maybe Karen's phone call was God's way of telling me *she* was the one instead. The thought of breaking up with Harriet plunged my heart into an abyss. But if I was to follow God's leading, I had to see clearly what He might be saying to me.

In addition, when I talked to my mother about the possibility of marrying Harriet, she gave me this warning: "You and Harriet come from very different backgrounds—Harriet is from a well-to-do family, and we are a minister's family. So realize that you are going to have to face that issue."

I wrestled with my dilemma for several days before I decided to contact an old friend and mentor. I laid my dilemma before him, and his simple answer surprised me.

"Go with Harriet," he said. "She and her family live right here in Texas. Karen is in Wisconsin, a two-day drive at least. Long-distance relationships seldom work. Stick with a Texas girl and you'll be with people, attitudes, and a culture you understand, not to mention a climate you enjoy. In Wisconsin you'll encounter a different culture and freezing weather. To you it will be like moving to a foreign country. Keep the Texas girl, Pete."

How strange, I thought. My friend's advice was based on practical stuff—nothing spiritual, nothing about compatibility, nothing involving the heart. But then I realized that when two options seem equally weighted in terms of relational and religious import, the practical considerations could legitimately tip the balance. He wiped the smoke from my eyes with simple, rational expedience.

I was delighted and relieved at my friend's advice. Breaking up with Harriet would have broken my heart. So I turned down Karen's invitation and went hunting with Harriet's dad.

৵৹

Our courtship was short. It only took four months for Harriet and me to know that we were right for each other. We knew we were a good fit. As we dug into each other's lives and asked the deeper questions, our instincts about each other became concrete. My faith and prayers had built my confidence to the point that I was ready to take a giant leap. So I took it:

"Will you marry me?"

"Yes!"

We were elated! For the next few days, Harriet and I floated on clouds of euphoria. We came back down to earth to meet with Harriet's parents and tell them we wanted to get married as soon as possible. We set a date two months away.

I was relieved her parents did not oppose the marriage. They loved their daughter dearly, and no doubt they could see how happy she was with me. But they did oppose our wedding date.

"We want to give you a proper wedding," explained her mother. "Two months simply doesn't give us enough time to make all the arrangements." Harriet's parents were well-to-do, and I had no doubt they had visions of a spectacular wedding for their only daughter.

"We strongly advise you to wait a year," added her father. "That will give your mom the time she needs to prepare for the wedding, and meanwhile Harriet can finish school."

I always wondered if, in addition to these two practical considerations, he had a hidden agenda. Ours had been a whirlwind courtship, and he may have felt that Harriet and I needed more time together to be sure of our relationship.

Heeding the wise counsel of Harriet's parents, we delayed our marriage for a year. Harriet and I sealed our commitment on June 15, 1968, in the church Harriet had grown up attending—St. Michaels and All Angels Episcopal Church in Dallas. It was a joyful ceremony and a beautiful beginning to our life together.

CHAPTER 2

OUR LIFE TOGETHER

To be able to profoundly influence another human being in a way that promotes a fulfilling awareness of their wholeness in Christ is a thrilling opportunity.

—LARRY CRABB, THE MARRIAGE BUILDER

I quickly learned that you don't marry an individual; you marry a family. We are products of our families, and our heritage from them includes both the good and the bad. The effects of the Fall that began with Adam and Eve brought a terrible disorder into Harriet's family—depression. Later I discovered that this mental illness had affected previous and present generations, including Harriet's father and grandmother. But in the early days of our marriage, we were happily oblivious to depression's impending shadow, with no inkling of the terrible blow it would inflict on us in the future.

Harriet and I built a wonderful life together. Our relationship was not perfect, of course. Like every marriage in this fallen world, ours had its normal ups and downs. But the overriding tenor of my life and love with Harriet was good and fruitful. We shared many fun travels, parties, friends, and the joys of our two daughters and eight grandchildren—all gifts from God. We also partnered in loving, teaching, and encouraging more people than I can count in five different cities, two great churches, and multiple countries. As I look back through the photo albums that document our life together, I am amazed at all the opportunities God gave us. Our journey together was nothing short of heavenly.

Yet it was a journey punctuated with deep lows of pain and bewilderment. Harriet and I suffered through the deaths of our grandparents, two siblings, several close friends, and eventually our parents. We wept over the deep pain of mistakes we made with our children and friends.

Three of these painful events significantly increased Harriet's struggle with depression. The first was the chaos of two unexpected job changes early in our marriage. After graduation, I accepted a position with the campus ministry we were involved in. This job required us to move twice in two years, first from Knoxville, Tennessee, to San Bernardino, California, and then from San Bernardino to Dallas, Texas. During one of our moves, Harriet was influenced by misguided mentors whose views about seeing the devil behind every bush kept her spiritual life out of balance, undermining her assurance while instilling fear and uncertainty.

The stress involved with these two moves was increased by the birth of our two daughters, which added to the buildup of Harriet's depression. Our young daughters brought us more joy than we ever dreamed possible; however, after the second baby, Harriet developed postpartum depression.

Naturally, I helped her all I could. I tried to come home early as often as my work allowed, and I got up often for night-time feedings. What I didn't realize at the time was that my help also contributed to her depression. She felt guilty that she was interrupting my work, which she considered to be very important. I didn't recognize that she had postpartum depression; I thought her mood swings were simply natural adjustments to our new routine. So neither I nor anyone else realized how much Harriet was struggling.

The third event that contributed to Harriet's depression was the dissolution of her parents' marriage. Their relationship had been deteriorating for years, but Harriet hadn't realized it because, in spite of their difficulties with each other, they both loved her deeply. In addition, she was away at college during the worst of their growing troubles.

We didn't know it at the time, but Harriet's father had planned to divorce her mother the week after our wedding. When we returned from our honeymoon, we discovered he had filed for divorce and was gone. He came back after a short period, only to leave again. The breakup of her parents' marriage blindsided Harriet, and she was devastated.

✿

Harriet wrestled with these issues for several years, but so many changes and traumas, coming one on top of the other, finally tipped the scales of her emotional equilibrium. The truth is, she was dealing with enough to throw anyone's life out of balance. The two quick major moves, my job changes, coping with two daughters under the age of three, and her parents' divorce aggravated her inherited condition and plunged Harriet into a deep depression that left her in hopeless despair.

One day I came home after work and found Harriet in our bedroom. She was huddled by the nightstand, weeping.

"Harriet, what on earth is wrong?" I asked.

"It's no use. I can't go on this way," she moaned.

She opened her hand; it was filled with sleeping pills. She moved her hand toward her mouth and reached for the glass of water on the nightstand.

"No!" I cried. I picked up the bottle, which had been full, and realized that she had already taken a hefty dose. She was beginning to pass out. In a panic, I somehow managed to get a neighbor to stay with the girls, help Harriet into the car, and rush her to the emergency room. They wasted no time pumping out her stomach, which saved her life.

This near-death experience was a wake-up call for all of us. Harriet's parents, though divorced, rallied around her. I was determined to get Harriet the best professional help available to prevent a recurrence of this kind of trauma. But we were dirt-poor at the time and could not afford what she needed. I didn't know how I was going to pull it off.

As I was searching for answers, her father came to me and said, "We cannot let this happen again. We've got to pull my little girl out of this. We must do whatever it takes—counseling, doctors, hospitals, medication—it doesn't matter. I'll pay for all of it. Just send me the bill."

Harriet's mother also stepped in. She had quickly recognized the seriousness of Harriet's depression and, I suspect, also realized that Harriet had inherited the family tendency toward it. It was why she had lobbied me to move back to Dallas after our second child was born, when she noted Harriet's postpartum struggle.

Thanks to her parents' love and generosity, Harriet received expert counsel and medical help that arrested the downward spiral. Over time, her doctors adjusted her psychiatric medication to the point that only a small dosage was required to level out the cycle of depression, enabling her to live a normal and fruitful life. By God's mercy, this regimen carried Harriet through the next thirty-eight years with only a minimal amount of struggle.

I learned later that Harriet's struggles with her inherited depression were also within the scope of God's plan. I cannot say that I understand everything about how they fit in, but I have to agree reluctantly with the words of that famous example of patient suffering, Job: "Shall we indeed accept good from God and not accept adversity?" (Job 2:10).

❧

Seeing the need for greater security in Harriet's life, I enrolled in Dallas Theological Seminary. I had never intended to leave campus ministry to become a pastor, but I could see that the travel, moves, and meager salary associated with campus ministry would not be conducive to her well-being. A seminary education would give me greater job security and, eventually, more financial stability as a pastor.

By God's grace, two of our longtime friends also decided to come to the same seminary at this time. Both were married and had kids the same age as ours. Our families became close and developed friendships that last to this day. This was a godsend for Harriet, in some ways as good as any medicine. She was not alone. She had mutual support and companionship to lean on and brighten her life. My time at DTS gave us a four-year period of stability and calm as well as a clearer path into the future.

Graduation from seminary launched us into wonderful years of new ministry, raising kids, and growing up together. We learned to trust each other deeply. We encouraged each other, helped each other, and even learned how to argue with each other.

Our church leaders asked us to teach classes on marriage. They were limited to twelve couples in order to encourage interaction. And did we ever have interaction! Ironically, Harriet and I had a fight at the beginning of one of the first classes. Talk about embarrassing! While driving to church to teach the class, we had gotten into an argument that left her mad as a hornet in a jar. Still angry when we arrived, she plopped down in a chair on the back row, arms folded, glaring at me across the room. Without my coteacher, I began leading the class alone.

"Tonight we will be talking about marriage problems," I began. "Never feel that your marriage is in trouble just because you encounter differences between yourselves. We all have problems. Harriet and I have our occasional problems."

Immediately Harriet's heated voice fired from the back, "We sure do!"

The class laughed and burst into applause. Someone said above the clapping, "Thank goodness, we've finally found a class where somebody's gonna be honest."

Another voice chimed in, "My wife and I also had an argument on the way to class tonight."

What a night that was! It showed that God can use even our fallen natures to further His glory. Our little tiff gave the group a glimpse of reality that completely changed the character of the class. Usually, wives want to come to marriage classes, but husbands have to be dragged along. But from that night on, our class was exceptionally well attended by both wives and husbands. They learned that all married couples struggle in the same way. Every marriage needs expert counsel, no matter how long a couple has been married. Yes, our marriage was made in heaven, but it had to be maintained on earth by flawed and fallen humans.

❧

Harriet's depression actually resulted in certain blessings to herself and others. It strengthened her resolve to understand what was going on inside her and to help others dealing with the same problems.

A close friend of Harriet's told me that she was ironing one day when Harriet called her. They had talked many times of her own personal struggles. Harriet knew her friend needed professional counseling, but she also knew that her friend wasn't taking any initiative at all in facing her issues. On this particular day, Harriet called her friend and said, "If you don't make an appointment with a counselor today, then I am going to do it for you!"

Harriet read every self-help book she could get her hands on and tried to do everything the authors recommended. This impossible task led to a period of constant frustration for her—and for our family as well. She followed the dietetic recommendations of those books to a fault, which meant I ate more health foods than I ever wanted—a desire that hovered at a minimal level to begin with. I will probably live to be 110 because of it (though I hope not). Everything we ate was whole-wheat something—whole-wheat pancakes, bread, doughnuts, and cereal (no sugar added, of course). Our poor daughters, Ginny and Ann, were put through the same regimen. Having been brought up on this diet, they didn't know there was such a thing as good-tasting food.

One day they accompanied their mother to a friend's house where the hostess passed around a plate of Oreo cookies. The girls looked hesitantly at their mother for approval, and in a weak moment, Harriet allowed the indulgence. They politely reached for a cookie and took their first bite. Their eyes lit up like sparklers! With a glorious expression of awe on her face, eight-year-old Ginny looked at her mom and exclaimed, "I've never in my life tasted anything so good!"

Harriet finally relaxed her health food obsession and gave it up. But not until God had used experiences like this to lead her into an amazing trust in Himself. And throughout the last decade of her life, He was her constant help.

Despite a few flare-ups of Harriet's depression, our family had many fun times together. As I mentioned, Harriet loved to play practical jokes. When our girls were in grade school, Harriet and our eight-year-old daughter, Ann, were planning a visit to a friend who had a strong distaste for animals or pets of any kind. Before they left, Harriet gave Ann a sealed plastic bag containing two small goldfish.

"Put this in your purse," she said, "and after we get to Linda's house, go to the restroom and dump these fish into the commode."

Ann did as she was told. Later in the visit, Linda went to the restroom. She came out with no doubt as to the identity of the guilty culprit and confronted Harriet accordingly.

"What did you do with the goldfish?" asked Harriet.

With her hands on her hips, Linda said, "I flushed them, of course. What else would you expect?"

I still don't know whether Harriet's guilt over the sad fate of those two innocent creatures overcame her delight in pulling off a successful practical joke. Somehow I doubt it.

Harriet's depression did not darken our marriage, but her rare flare-ups did bring a certain imbalance to our relationship. Her episodes caused me to assume the role of a protector, which was both good and bad. The good part was that it strengthened my manhood. The bad part was that it weakened my appreciation of her femininity. It was fine with Harriet for me to be her knight in shining armor, but she did not want to be seen as a damsel in continual distress. It made her think that I saw her as weak.

Our last ten years as empty nesters were wonderful. We discovered new intimacy, new friends, and new travels. We complemented each other more than ever. We discovered a new gift of freedom and creativity in our marriage. We let each other flourish in new ways.

Harriet discovered a creative outlet and talent in flowers. She made a blooming business out of it (pardon the pun) and won many awards for her creations. She soon learned, however, that it wasn't the business side of flower arranging that gave her satisfaction; it was the exercise of her God-given talent for creating beauty.

She was a member of the Founders Garden Club (FGC), which is associated with the prestigious Garden Club of America. Through her participation in the FGC, she was eligible to enter national floral arrangement competitions. No doubt her finest achievement in this area was twice winning first place in the national Most Creative Arrangement category—a feat rarely accomplished by any Dallas member. She was presented a plaque bearing this inscription: "The Harriet DeWaele Puckett Award presented to Harriet Deison by the Garden Club of America in recognition of skill in a unique tasteful and creative response to a challenging flower arrangement schedule." In addition, her arrangement also won Best in Show.

But the year 2000 brought a new challenge. Harriet developed ulcerative colitis, a debilitating and painful disease that can be fatal. Doctors told her that the only cure was the surgical removal of her entire colon and wearing a colostomy bag for the rest of her life. This was no small decision, and one that neither Harriet nor I wanted to make.

"At what point should I have this done?" she asked her doctor.

"I can't tell you that," he replied. "But I assure you, there will come a time when you will want me to take out the offending organ."

Her condition grew more and more unbearable. The pain and continual diarrhea brought her to the point that it became almost impossible for her to go out of the house to do ordinary things such as buying groceries or visiting friends. Finally, she felt there was no alternative.

"It's time," she said.

The colon was removed. The upside was that she was free of the pain and bowel issues. The downside was that she had to wear a colostomy bag—a small pouch just below the right side of her stomach. The lack of a colon led to many adjustments in her diet, yet neither the food limitations nor the bag slowed her down or triggered more depression. I can truly and thankfully say that she was more beautiful during the last decade of her life than when I first met her.

I have long been convinced that God had a purpose in allowing Harriet to be afflicted by such major medical problems. Coping with those health issues engaged her natural capacity for empathy and gave her opportunities for a ministry of encouragement to others who struggled with personal challenges, especially depression.

Even as a young child, encouraging others was as natural to Harriet as breathing. One day when her brother, Hugo, was sick and had to stay home from school, Harriet decided to dance around in a grass hula skirt to make him laugh. In the middle of a twirl, her hula skirt brushed a wall heater and caught fire.

She spent the next ten years having skin grafts, and she bore scars on her back until the day she died. But that experience gave Harriet a keen ability to sense other people's pain. She was by anyone's witness the most empathetic, compassionate, tender-hearted person they had ever known. God used her to minister gently to those she found in pain wherever we lived. She delighted in encouraging others, and people of all ages continually sought her out.

One friend explained that Harriet had saved her life. "I, too, suffered from depression," she said, "and it had become so severe that I was sliding into a deep hole. But she understood what I was going through, and through her love and encouragement, I sought professional help and pulled out of it."

Her husband said, "Harriet also saved our marriage. My wife's depression was creating a barrier between us that I did not know how to overcome."

This is just one example of the many lives Harriet influenced. She often used her intense personal struggles to encourage others. She was not embarrassed by her depression and was willing to talk about it with most people. She didn't parade her affliction; rather, she learned to use it. She frequently said her struggle drew her closer to God. And hundreds of people can attest that God used her mightily to bless other strugglers.

CHAPTER 3

AN EARTH-SHATTERING INSTANT

There is no pit so deep, but He is not deeper still.
—CORRIE TEN BOOM, *THE HIDING PLACE*

Harriet's struggle with depression intensified in the late fall of 2012. She expressed concern that the medications she was taking to control the clinical depression she had battled most of her adult life were not working as they should. Her doctor prescribed new medications designed to be more effective and took her off the previous ones. He explained that it would take the new drugs a month or more to achieve their full effect.

During the difficult few weeks between medications, Harriet experienced several panic attacks that gave her an irresistible compulsion to run and hide. These attacks were so severe that I even slept by our bedroom door to hold her and help her calm down when she tried to run. I remember one particular night, we sat on the bed and I prayed for what seemed like hours. She said, "You are my rock." I held her hand until she finally drifted back to sleep. The doctors kept saying this darkness would soon lift, and she accepted that. We both believed that life would soon return to normal.

The new medications made Harriet drowsy, which rendered driving and other daily activities dangerous or impossible. The doctor thought a change in the timing of the dosage would solve the problem. I was watching the entire process closely and monitoring Harriet's condition, activities, and medication regimen.

On Saturday, December 29, 2012—four days after Christmas— Harriet woke up earlier than normal and said she felt better. She loved to swim and usually went to the Y every day to swim with friends. I had not been letting her drive because of the drowsiness, but that morning she felt so good that she wanted to drive herself. I saw her request as a hopeful sign that the new meds were taking hold, but I was not ready to hand over the keys until I was sure. So I rode with her to the Y and worked out with the StairMaster and weights while she swam with her friends. Several of them told me later that Harriet's conversations with them had been normal and upbeat. They, too, saw signs that she was emerging from her darkness.

When we returned home, Harriet told me that if she was still feeling well later in the day, she wanted to go to the wedding of a close friend. Further evidence that she had turned a corner was that she also called two friends to come over for a visit early that afternoon.

Another event that I took as good news was that she asked if she could drive to a nearby shopping center and get her hair done for the wedding. All signs pointed to the fact that she was ready to handle the car, so I let her take it. She came back an hour later, upbeat and confident as she always seemed to be when she got her hair done. I was elated. I felt sure she was getting back to normal. The new medications were finally doing their job.

But my elation was premature. We sat down to eat lunch, and she fell asleep at the table. When I roused her, she complained of feeling terrible. I took her to the bedroom, laid her down, and gave her half of a pill that the doctor had prescribed to help her rest.

"How do you feel now?" I asked.

"Very, very dark," she said. Her voice sounded far away.

"Just rest for now. If you don't feel better soon, I'll call the doctor."

"Would you put some hymns on the CD player?" she asked. I did as she requested, and she put her earphones on to listen and rest.

"Wake me up when my friends come," she mumbled as her drowsiness deepened.

I watched as she began to relax. "Don't worry, sweetheart," I said. "We'll make it through this."

"Do you promise?"

"I promise." And I truly believed what I said. We were almost at the six-week point where the doctors expected the new meds to take hold.

Those were our last words to each other.

I went into my office to prepare my sermon for the next day. Forty-five minutes later I went to check on Harriet. She was not in her bed. Where could she have gone? I searched the house, but she was nowhere to be found. I had left the car keys on the kitchen counter; they were missing. My heart began to race. I rushed to the garage. Her car was gone. I panicked. My office was only thirty feet away from where the keys were; how had I missed hearing her leave the room and walk out of the house? Where could she have gone?

My first impulse was to jump in my car and go after her. I had no idea which direction she might have gone, but that didn't stop me. I had to find her before her drowsy condition caused a crash.

My search was frantic. I went everywhere I thought she might have gone—including the pharmacy, the grocery store, and the beauty shop. I was about to call the police when my cell phone rang. It was the police calling me. They had found Harriet's car on Garland Road. My heart jumped into my throat; I was sure she had been in an accident. I was eager to go to her, but the policeman would not tell me where the car was or what had happened. Now distraught, I pleaded with him to tell me something.

"Hold on," he replied. "Let me get my supervisor."

I waited and waited, pressing my phone hard against my ear. Minutes passed, but the supervisor never came on. I could hear traffic in the background. What could have happened? Why was the car out there? Why wouldn't the officer tell me anything?

Finally, he came back on the line and said, "I'm going to have to call you right back."

I was beside myself. I could not just sit there and wait. I determined to drive along Garland Road and find the car myself. I drove for what seemed hours (though it was nothing like that long) up and down the twenty-mile-long road, and my distress was pushing me well over the speed limit. But I never saw Harriet's car or the police. The longer I waited for the call, the more I knew the news must be bad. Was it a car wreck? I called 911 repeatedly, but they had no information. Fear flooded my mind. I was fighting it and crying all the while.

Finally, the call came. "Mr. Deison, please drive to your house, and a police officer will meet you there."

At that moment, I knew the news would be the worst. I don't

know how I got home or even saw the road through my tears. Yet I got there, still having no idea what had happened. Two detectives arrived shortly afterward, and after settling me into a chair, they gave me the news I dreaded to hear:

"Mr. Deison, your wife is dead."

The terrible words hit me with such impact that I went numb with shock. I couldn't put my thoughts together. Questions as sharp as shattered glass ravaged my mind: *How could she be dead? What could possibly have happened to her? How will I ever get through this?*

The two policemen carefully explained the results of their investigation. Harriet had driven to a gun store, purchased a handgun, gotten back into her car in the parking lot, and pulled the trigger. My beautiful Harriet—full of compassion for those who hurt, wife of a pastor, mother of two lovely daughters, grandmother of eight fun grandkids, and a prizewinner of floral designs—was gone from this world in one earth-shattering instant.

❧

From that moment to the time of Harriet's funeral, I felt like a zombie. Almost fifteen hundred people attended the funeral. The flowers were magnificently designed by her favorite florist, who insisted on gifting them out of love for Harriet. The service was a beautiful blur. I was there, yet I wasn't. I may have been in shock, but I was far from numb. I felt pain as I had never felt it before.

I cried at almost every turn and found that my tears were of two kinds. Many were the obvious tears of loss, but I also cried at every tender act of friendship and compassion toward me. At first it bothered me that I could not control my emotions, especially when they were tears of gratitude. Then I realized that crying is part of grief. My tears have since slowed down, but they haven't stopped. A part of my heart was ripped open the day Harriet died, and that wound will never be fully closed this side of heaven. Tears come because scar tissue is more sensitive to the touch. I have learned to live with that sensitivity and to embrace my tears and the fact that people accept them.

For weeks, almost everyone's question to me was, "How are you doing, Pete?" It was a difficult question to answer. One moment I was okay, and the next I was in agony. In order to respond honestly, I began to give this answer: "I have two responses to your question: The first is, I am a little better. The second is, I don't know how I am doing. I've never been here before."

I've discovered that everyone grieves differently, so there are no standards or boundaries to tell you where you are in the recovery process. You simply keep moving forward with the tasks that are in front of you.

❧

No one saw Harriet's suicide coming. Two nights before her death, she wrote an e-mail to a friend in which she admitted that she was struggling with doubt but believed she was turning the corner. She even had an affirming conversation with her spiritual mentor the night before she took her life. To all who knew Harriet, loved her, and needed her, Harriet's suicide made little sense.

The immediate clinical cause, I believe, was clear. Her death was precipitated by a combination of new medications not providing the needed "base of coverage" (as doctors described it), which meant the old medicines lost their effectiveness before the new ones had developed strength in her system. This imbalance resulted in tremendous highs and lows of both anxiety and depression in her last days. The doctors did the best they could do. Everyone thought she would make it.

But I searched for deeper answers than these clinical explanations provided. I could not sleep. I kept going over the last days of her life—how the tragedy happened, why it happened, and what could have been different.

Harriet could have found a way of escape on that fateful day—there were several possible sources she could have turned to. I was nearby. Some dear friends who nurtured and embraced her with unconditional love had planned to spend the afternoon with us. She could have waited for their support before plunging into fatal despair. In addition, she had time to reconsider the irrevocable act during the twenty-minute drive to the gun shop and the discussion she had with the store clerk. Why didn't Harriet reach out for these lifelines? It's a question I have asked myself time and time again.

I am certain that on that day she did not have full mental control. Her mind was saturated with the darkness of her depression, which smothered her capacity to reason. And certainly Satan, the dark enemy of our souls, was taking every advantage of Harriet's weakness.

I was left with resounding questions: *How do I understand Harriet's death? Who and what are responsible? Where is God in all this?*

Driven by the insatiable desire to understand Harriet's death, I read widely in the Scriptures and pored over books about heaven, angels, near-death experiences, and grief. I endured long days and nights of soul searching and coping with pain.

One of my most urgent questions centered on the fact that Harriet took her own life. For many Christians, there is a stigma attached to suicide. Taking one's own life is considered to be one of the most grievous of sins—unforgivable in the minds of many. I could not let the question rest. I dug into the Bible for answers.

❦

My study of the Bible made it clear that suicide is not an option for anyone—especially a Christian—to use as the way out of a problem.

Among the Ten Commandments that God gave Moses was "You shall not murder" (Exodus 20:13). This principle applies to suicide because suicide is self-murder. Murder destroys what God has created. His reason for this command went deeper than simply to provide stability in a civil society. It is much more sacred. God reminded Noah that the life of a person reflects God's image (Genesis 9:6), which means that taking life destroys God's highest creation.

Suicide is also an extreme act of dishonoring God with one's body. Since the Bible tells us that our bodies are temples of the Holy Spirit (1 Corinthians 6:19), we are dishonoring the Holy Spirit when we destroy the body.

Further, suicide violates the biblical assertion that there is a way of escape from every temptation. Paul wrote that God "will not allow you to be tempted beyond what you are able, but with the temptation will provide the way of escape" (1 Corinthians 10:13).

Suicide negatively affects the plans of God in creating a believer for good works. "For we are His workmanship, created in Christ Jesus for good works, which God prepared beforehand so that we would walk in them" (Ephesians 2:10). When issues tempt or cause a person to consider suicide, that person becomes self-focused, with an inward perspective only. The outward perspective of seeking to do good for God's glory is lost.

Finally, suicide robs the believer of future rewards in heaven by cutting days on earth shorter than God intended. While our works don't earn us a place in heaven, Scripture makes it clear that they do increase our rewards, as Jesus noted in the parable of the talents (Matthew 25). The Gospels mention rewards more than seventy times, and Paul affirmed the concept of heavenly rewards for earthly work: "If any man's work which he has built on it remains, he will receive a reward" (1 Corinthians 3:14).

These verses confirm that God sees every struggle, when faced with faith, as valuable. The act of suicide diminishes the opportunities a believer has to do good things for God's glory.

The Bible leaves no doubt that taking one's own life is a sin. God has ordained our days (Psalm 139:16). He has a plan and reason for every day of our lives.

❧

My study on suicide provided much clarity but little comfort. Big questions remained: *Who or what was ultimately responsible for Harriet's death?* And again, *Where was God in all this?* My struggle for understanding continued. *The Bible promises God will provide us a way of escape, so where was Harriet's escape? Why didn't she take it?*

At that point, the God of light and peace brought two people into my life whose words spoke volumes to me and set me on a course of discovery.

One night while I was working late at the church, a young man knocked on my office window. I recognized him as a member of our church, so I let him in. He introduced himself and said he had felt a strong compulsion, which he believed to be from God, to talk to me about his own struggle with depression. I invited him to sit down and share his story.

"I have battled deep depression all my adult life," he said. "I've even been on suicide watch twice. People who haven't experienced it can't possibly imagine the darkness of that horrible place depression puts us in. It's like being in hell. When a person falls into it, escaping the pain becomes all-consuming. The depressed person wants nothing but to get out. Thoughts of escape dominate the mind, and without help a person will become desperate enough to take any exit that presents itself—even death." He paused to let that sink in and then added, "I completely understand why Harriet did it."

The second interaction came by way of professional counselor Ron Rolheiser. His analysis may not apply to every case of suicide, but it is true of suicide deaths linked to depression, Harriet's included.

A person dying of suicide dies as does a victim of physical illness or accident, against his or her will. People die from physical heart attacks, strokes, cancer, AIDS and accidents. Death by suicide is the same, except that we are dealing with an emotional heart attack, an emotional stroke, emotional AIDS, emotional cancer and an emotional fatality.[1]

The wisdom shared by these two individuals was helpful and comforting because it helped me better understand the victim of clinical depression. These insights pointed me in the right direction, but peace was yet some distance away. I begged God to grant me further understanding, and in time and through my continued search of the Scriptures, He did. I was able to come to peace about Harriet's death through several verses the Lord opened to me.

The first, Exodus 4:10–11, occurs just after God commanded Moses to go to Egypt, confront Pharaoh, and lead Israel out of bondage. Moses told God that he was not a good speaker and therefore could not do what God was asking. God replied, in essence, "Who makes the mute? Who makes the deaf? Who makes the blind? Is it not I, the Lord?" Through these words, I realized God takes responsibility for what He gives us. God could have continued by saying, "Who makes the depressed?" Why do some people have clinical depression and others don't? It is because God creates people with both abilities and disabilities that serve His purposes.

The second Bible verse God opened to me was Job 42:11. After God had confronted Job for his lack of understanding, Job's family brought gifts to console him "for all the adversities that the LORD had brought on him." God had allowed the adversities that Job experienced. God is sovereign and never loses control.

In putting together these two Bible verses, my questions regarding who was responsible for Harriet's death were answered. *God takes responsibility.* He made Harriet with her particular disability, and for His all-knowing purposes, He allowed Satan to take advantage of her weakened condition.

When I placed what I had learned in context, it felt as if God were saying, *Pete, I was with Harriet the whole time. I could have stopped her death, yet I allowed it for My reasons. Trust Me with what you do not understand right now. Harriet is with Me, fulfilling new purposes I have for her.*

This can be true of death by cancer, accidents, or even old age. God never leaves us. He doesn't always explain His ways, but He does explain His care.

After I had reached the point of biblically understanding and accepting my wife's death, I was free of the mental trap of placing blame, agonizing over her future, or running in perpetual circles seeking answers to why.

In the mystery and beauty of God's grace, suicide is not an unforgivable sin. How could God ordain a deficiency in a person and then condemn him for having it? Scripture makes clear that the only unforgivable sin is rejecting the Holy Spirit by refusing to accept Christ's sacrifice for your sins (Matthew 12:31). Suicide, like all other sins, receives God's forgiveness.

It took me about three months of prayer and seeking God to come to this conclusion. During this process, unusual things began happening that I could not explain. I am by nature a logic-driven and rational person, trained to use a biblical framework to explain everything. Soon after Harriet's death, however, events began to unfold that did not fit my theological worldview, driving me to dig deep to understand their meaning from a biblical outlook. My understanding of heaven, Harriet's presence there, and my relationship with her were about to change in a dramatic, eye-opening way.

PART 2

THE ROAD BACK
TO LIFE

CHAPTER 4

HEAVEN'S COMPASSION

If any or all of them are at times sent on errands of duty
or mercy to distant worlds, or employed, as some suppose
them to be, as ministering spirits to friends in this world,
they are still led by the influence of love to conduct, in
all their behavior, in such a manner as is well pleasing
to God, and thus conducive to their own and others'
happiness.

JONATHAN EDWARDS, *CHARITY AND ITS FRUITS*

On the morning of January 21, 2013, three weeks after Harriet's death, I was awakened by the sound of hymns playing. I crawled out of bed, wondering if I had absentmindedly left the television on the night before. But the screen in the den stared back at me, dark and mute.

The hymns, however, kept floating through the house like prayers. I finally traced them to the dining room, and there I found the source: Harriet's cell phone. I stood there, stunned. I had carried my wife's phone around with me for three long weeks. It had remained silent except for the times when I played her recorded message just to once again hear the melody of her sweet voice.

But on that cold January day, hymns were playing on her phone, and they warmed my heart. After closer inspection, I realized the hymns were set as Harriet's wake-up alarm tone. I laughed, because it felt as if God had allowed Harriet to nudge me awake with joyful noise and then hug me. She loved the old hymns and often hummed them as she arranged flowers. I listened a few moments longer, and then I turned off the alarm feature. I praised God for His tender mercy and began my day with a smile for the first time since her death.

The next morning it happened again. I was awakened by the powerful lyrics and melody of the hymn "Be Thou My Vision" emanating from Harriet's cell phone.

> *Be Thou my vision, O Lord of my heart;*
> *Naught be all else to me, save that Thou art,*
> *Thou my best Thought, by day or by night,*
> *Walking or sleeping, Thy presence my light.*[1]

I grabbed my glasses, rechecked Harriet's phone settings, and discovered that the morning alarm was set. *That's odd*, I thought. I was sure I had disabled the alarm feature the day before. Even more puzzling, the alarm was set to go off at 6:44 a.m., and it was only 6:30. At the time, I laughed it off and chalked it up to odd things cell phones do. But I soon discovered that this wasn't a technical fluke at all. Far from it. It was the beginning of many events that would convince me that my merciful and loving God was allowing Harriet to communicate with me from her new home in heaven.

At this point, I know this assertion must seem unusual. You are probably thinking that in my distraught state, I was interpreting ordinary occurrences through the filter of my lonely grief and making them into something more than they were. But before you make such a judgment, please read on.

THE BIRTHDAY LETTER

The first of these cell phone incidents occurred three days before my birthday. It was a day I dreaded because Harriet had always made birthdays special for me. On the day before, I opened my mail and found a card from a longtime family friend who lives in Chattanooga. It featured a beautifully designed presentation of the apostle Paul's prayer from Ephesians 3: "Now to Him who is able to do far more abundantly beyond all that we ask or think, according to the power that works within us" (v. 20).

She had added this note:

Pete, I know this is an especially hard birthday for you without Harriet, but I am praying for God to bless you above and beyond.

And He did.

On the following day, my birthday, I received a letter from another of Harriet's longtime friends. Within the envelope was a smaller envelope, turning brown at the edges and containing another letter. Before opening that obviously older envelope, I read our friend's note:

Pete, I had no idea why I kept this letter for forty-five years, but when I reread it after Harriet's death, I knew the answer. I kept it for you.

With trembling fingers, I opened the second envelope. Within it was a handwritten letter from Harriet—one she had written to her friend about me forty-five years earlier. We had just become engaged at the time, and Harriet wrote the letter to express her elation:

> I want to tell you about this wonderful man God has brought into my life. . . .

Then Harriet wrote two pages about me, including this paragraph that made my heart soar:

> I saw him . . . and could not take my eyes off him. It's not necessarily his good looks—mainly it's the radiating love and strength in Jesus that is so obvious in his face and his continual joy! That night, I went to my room and wrote a prayer, telling the Lord I thought Pete was the boy He had picked out for me, and if Pete were that boy, it would be up to the Lord to bring us together, and He did!

I was blown away! My friend's "above and beyond" prayer in the letter I received the day before was answered in a way that only God could orchestrate. Harriet's friend found Harriet's saved letter in a box of keepsakes and sent it to me. She had no way to know I would receive it on my birthday.

Why then? Why did I receive a forty-five-year-old love letter on my sixty-seventh birthday? I recalled the hymns that had emanated so victoriously from Harriet's cell phone, especially "Be Thou My Vision." I also thought about the "above and beyond" prayer that presaged Harriet's letter. And that is when the heaven where Harriet now lives began to feel like a place I could truly imagine. I was beginning to find solid footing where before I'd been stumbling around in grief. It was also the first time I knew without a doubt that God was allowing Harriet, ever the encourager, to work in heaven on my behalf.

God knew how deeply I would grieve Harriet's death and how she would be concerned for me. Perhaps He told Harriet something like this: "Harriet, forty-five years ago you wrote a letter to a friend and told her about Pete. I had her keep that letter all this time so she would send it to Pete to arrive on his birthday like a love letter from you."

The hymns and Harriet's letter were just the beginning of the tender visits of compassion that would flow to me from heaven in the coming months and years—visits that sealed my belief that Harriet still loves me, still prays for me, and is reaching out to me as God allows.

WRITTEN IN THE BOOKS

Harriet was an avid reader. She frequently read a book a week. One lonely afternoon after her death, I was going through her bookshelves looking for a copy of John Claypool's *Tracks of a Fellow Struggler*.[2] It is probably the best book ever written on grief. I had read it years earlier. To my surprise, I found not only that book but also three others written by Claypool: *The Hopeful Heart*, *Mending the Heart*, and *God Is an Amateur*.[3]

As I sat in Harriet's office reading through those books, I quickly realized that she had marked them in exact places that answered questions I was asking myself that day. One book had a scrap of paper protruding from its pages flagging a story about people reuniting in heaven. The paper was yellowed and had obviously been there for years. An underlined sentence in the story read, "The One who gave me 'the good old days' so graciously can be trusted to give me good new days as well."[4] I wept tears of joy. In Claypool's book *The Hopeful Heart*, Harriet had marked the following line: "The worst things are never the last things in the hands of God's ingenious mercy."[5]

Once again I felt God graciously allowing Harriet to speak to me, giving me the encouragement I needed to walk this earth without her physically by my side. I was strengthened by the ever-growing awareness that Harriet, by God's grace, was actively helping me grieve.

A VALENTINE FROM HARRIET

Early on the morning of February 14, 2013, six weeks after Harriet's death, I thought again about how much I missed her as I realized that there would be no tender card from her on Valentine's Day, no love message written in her unique script. I had the blues on a day adorned with red.

At 6:00 a.m., our wonderful housekeeper, Maria, whom Harriet cherished, arrived, and we discussed the housekeeping tasks for the day. As I was heading out to teach a Bible study, a thought came to me: *Give Maria a valentine.*

Time and time again, Harriet had modeled a particular and effective practice: to shake off the blues, choose to do something for someone else. I decided to imitate my thoughtful wife. I didn't have a Valentine's Day card, and giving money didn't seem appropriate. So I went into my office in search of a gift for Maria. Out of the corner of my eye, I saw something small and red on the top shelf of my bookcase. I stretched to get it and in the process knocked something else over. The red item was a small leather-bound book written by Henry Drummond titled *The Greatest Thing in the World,*[6] which is based on 1 Corinthians 13. I thought the book would be an appropriate Valentine's Day gift for Maria, who models selfless hard work and tender mercy. I tucked it under my arm and then reached up to see what I had knocked over while reaching for the book. To my amazement, it was the Valentine's Day card Harriet had given me the year before. I did not recall placing it on my bookcase. I opened the card and joyfully read the printed words. But it was Harriet's handwritten note that thrilled me:

> Honey, I love you so & thank you for your love & devotion & protection.

Never had fifteen words, especially her comment about protection, meant so much. God, the author of love, once again allowed Harriet to make her vibrant presence known and let me know that her love would last forever.

An Appearance at the New York Yacht Club

Harriet loved weddings. Before Christmas 2012 she had reminded me to make our plane reservations to New York for her cousin's March wedding at the New York Yacht Club. Harriet and I had never been to New York City together, and she was looking forward to the trip. (Her anticipation of this wedding was another confirmation that Harriet's suicide was unplanned.)

In Harriet's absence, our younger daughter, Ann, attended the wedding with me. The facilities of the New York Yacht Club are stunning. The main room features floor-to-ceiling hand-carved wood. A giant carved-stone fireplace vaults upward in the center of the room. Pictures of famous yachts of club members cover the walls in every room, some going back to the early 1800s. As we admired the beauty of the place, we turned to each other and said almost simultaneously, "Oh, Mom would love this!"

Ann then excused herself to go to the powder room. Moments later she returned, her face flushed with excitement. "Dad, you will not believe what I just saw!" she said. "They have pictures of yachts even in the restrooms. As I was washing my hands, I looked up and directly in front of me was a yacht named *The Harriet*. She is here, Dad. Mom is here!"

Ann's assertion made sense. Harriet would not have missed this wedding. In fact, her last visit with the bride, her niece, was on Christmas Day, and the two had discussed how the wedding flowers should look. After the wedding, we learned that the bride had arranged them exactly as Harriet had suggested.

Hymns playing on a cell phone; a forty-year-old love letter; specific lines marked in books; a Valentine's Day card that spoke of her love; a picture indicating her presence in the New York City Yacht Club. These incidents were all so compassionate, so encouraging, so like Harriet. Each added to my growing awareness that she is living a vibrant life in heaven. I realized that in His tender mercy, God was orchestrating these events. He was allowing Harriet to reach out to me with tender encouragement.

Is it possible that these happenings were mere coincidences that I chose to interpret as evidences of Harriet's presence? Or were they what I thought them to be—signs deliberately sent from heaven to earth to assure me of Harriet's continued reality and care?

I found the answer in a letter C. S. Lewis wrote to his friend Sheldon Vanauken, who was, like me, grieving the loss of his wife. Vanauken had seen a brilliant rainbow as a God-sent sign of hope that seemed to have significant personal meaning in relation to his wife's death. Fearing that the meaning he assigned to the rainbow was merely a product of his imagination interacting with his grief, he wrote Lewis for an answer. Lewis assured him that God is not indifferent to our situation and allows ordinary events of nature to encourage us.[7]

In other words, nothing that occurs by God's hand is accidental or coincidental. He knows in advance all the effects that every event will have on those who experience it, and those effects are part of His intention and examples of His providence in action.

In his book *God Is an Amateur*, John Claypool reminds us that we should not limit the reality of God to the audible. "I want to add the category of timeliness and appropriateness to this whole phenomenon and suggest that whenever something occurs that fits our need the way a key fits a lock, this too should be regarded as a form of God's 'speaking' to us or dealing with us."[8]

But what I've related to you so far is merely a prelude. The occurrences that opened my eyes to the light and life that truly shines from Harriet's new heavenly home are yet to be told. They came in the form of vivid dreams (mine and those of others) that left no doubt that heaven and earth are touching and the doors between them are not closed. The chapter you are about to read communicates these dreams and other experiences that are mine alone because of God's grace, but I pray that these events and encounters will encourage you as you make your way along the path of grief. It is through vivid dreams that I discovered that Harriet is active in heaven—and still using the spiritual gifts and talents she used for God's glory on earth.

CHAPTER 5

WHEN THE DREAM GATE OPENED

Indeed God speaks once, or twice, yet no one notices it. In a dream, a vision of the night, when sound sleep falls on men, while they slumber in their beds, then He opens the ears of men, and seals their instruction.

—JOB 33:14–16

At the turn of the twentieth century, the existence of heaven was far more accepted than it is today. Advances in science and technology have shifted our vision to a materialistic perception of reality and blinded us to greater and more solid realities that don't register on scientific instruments. These realities are faith driven; they surround and undergird heaven and the lives our loved ones embrace after they leave earth. Just because these realities cannot be empirically proven, observed by telescopes, confirmed by scientific methods, or pulled up on a smartphone app does not mean they are not real. Indeed, we have excellent reasons for believing that the reality we call heaven is even more real and more solid than the reality we experience in the material realm. We have increasing clarity that the lives our departed loved ones enjoy in this realm are vibrant, close, and personal, and that they remain closely connected to those they love on earth. The doors and windows between our reality and theirs are not closed.

We see this in the story of Abraham. Scripture says that when God observed events in Abraham's life, God spoke from heaven to those involved (Genesis 21:17; 22:10–11).

In 1850 Henry Edward Cardinal Manning described the reality our departed Christian loved ones know in heaven:

> Let us, then, learn, first of all, that we can never be lonely or forsaken in this life. . . .
>
> Shall they forget us because they are "made perfect"? Shall they love us the less because they now have power to love us more? If we forget them not, shall they not remember us with God?
>
> No trial, then, can isolate us; no sorrow can cut us off from the Communion of Saints. . . .
>
> Kneel down, and you are with them; lift your eyes, and the heavenly world, high above all perturbation, hangs serenely overhead; only a thin veil, it may be, floats between. . . . All whom we loved, and all who loved us; whom we still love no less, while they love us yet more, are ever near, because ever in His presence in whom we live and dwell.[1]

Grief often makes the reality Cardinal Manning described as difficult to grasp as smoke. Questions come far more readily than answers. As soon as death darkens our door, the questions flow. These questions are intense and acutely honest, and they will not go away. *Does she still know me? Love me? Is she aware of my existence? Can she communicate with me?* Yet because we fear what the answers might be, we often keep such questions to ourselves.

When Harriet died, I began to ask myself the questions I dared not pose to others. My most pressing questions I inadvertently addressed to Harriet herself: *Harriet, can you hear me?* My internal questions soon became consistently addressed to her. And shortly afterward they became external conversations—one-way verbal chats based on my sincere belief that Harriet was still near me. I surmised that I could not lose a soul mate with whom I shared forty-five years of life and not sense her closeness, as fragrant as perfume. Physically I knew she was gone, but spiritually I felt her presence. Grief creates that alcove.

Often I found myself engaged in a conversation with Harriet almost without being aware: *Honey, I remember when we bought that picture. Do you recall the fun of that day?* On and on the one-way conversations went—so frequently, in fact, that I began to wonder if I were going crazy. But I was soon to find that I was not. In days to come, I would learn beyond all doubt that death had not broken the connection between Harriet and me. The communication lines between heaven and earth were open and active.

THE REALITY FOUND IN DREAMS

A few weeks after Harriet's death, I drove to a small cabin she and I had built in the country for our family to enjoy. I needed to know if I could still find rest and peace there without her. By God's grace, I was greeted not with sorrow but with hope, for that night I had the most vivid dream I have ever had. It was unlike any dream I had ever experienced. I soon found that this dream was a prelude to a completely new phase of my existence. It was the first of many dreams yet to come. The odd thing about this is that before this time I had never been much of a dreamer.

Anyone who has been married will understand the value and intent in my first dream about Harriet because it was filled with romance. So you will appreciate why I don't divulge the details. I was not sure what to make of the dream, except that it reflected my longing for her. Yet it also included her encouragement toward me. I saw this as a wonderful, one-time dream and pondered often on its meaning. But it wasn't until I had two more dreams that I began to believe they were real-life communications with Harriet that God, in His tender mercy, was allowing from heaven.

The second dream occurred on March 8, 2013. On their spring break, my daughter Ann, her husband, and their four sons were visiting me, and together we went to our family's cabin. The first night we were there, extreme sadness engulfed me the entire evening. Harriet and I had built the cabin specifically to experience family togetherness—to enjoy time there with our daughters, sons-in-law, and grandkids. But Harriet's absence from the family circle created a vast chasm in my sense of togetherness, and I lost myself in it.

That night I had another dream. It was far from romantic yet vibrantly real. In the dream, Harriet entered the cabin and got right in my face. She was sweating as if she had been working outside in the heat. In life I rarely saw Harriet sweat, but in this dream her skin was wet and glistening. But she looked at me with such peace, and she was radiant and joyful.

Then she said, "Pete, enjoy the cabin and ranch with our family; that is why we built it."

Harriet's words released my sadness. And her tender focus on me during the dream later reminded me of a quote from F. Scott

Fitzgerald's book *The Great Gatsby* that a close friend of ours had shared with me:

> He smiled understandingly—much more than understandingly. It was one of those rare smiles with a quality of eternal reassurance in it, that you may come across four or five times in life. It faced—or seemed to face—the whole eternal world for an instant, and then concentrated on *you* with an irresistible prejudice in your favor. It understood you just as far as you wanted to be understood, believed in you as you would like to believe in yourself, and assured you that it had precisely the impression of you that, at your best, you hoped to convey.[2]

That passage beautifully captures the essence of Harriet's gaze into my eyes as I witnessed it in my dream.

Not long after that cabin trip, I had another dream. Harriet and I were in our first apartment in Austin, Texas. I had never dreamed about this apartment, and frankly, it wasn't a place to dream about.

In the dream, I was sitting in a chair, and Harriet walked in completely unclothed and pushed a vacuum cleaner toward me. Almost instantly I understood the import of the dream. She was naked so I could see that the colostomy bag she had worn for the last fifteen years of her life was gone. There was no port in the skin, no scar, no evidence that she had ever worn or needed the bag. She was beautiful, perfect, flawless. It was as if she were trying to tell me, "Pete, I am whole, and I am still yours."

At first the vacuum cleaner puzzled me, but then I realized the meaning of it. Early in our marriage, vacuuming was often my household chore. In the dream, she was bringing the machine back to me as a symbol to tell me that it was time to take up my responsibilities again. I realized she was saying, "You need to get on with life. I am still here with you, but you have responsibilities."

It was at that point I realized each dream was coming at the precise time in my life when I needed specific words of encouragement. These dreams further supported my growing belief that Harriet was still close by and could hear me as God allowed.

I continued my quest to know more about heaven, studying the Scriptures and many faith-centered books, including *The Business of Heaven* by C. S. Lewis, *The Heaven Answer Book* by Billy Graham, *Heaven* by Joni Eareckson Tada, *Heaven Revealed* by Paul Enns, and *Heaven* by Randy Alcorn.[3] Through my studies, I came to understand that in heaven Harriet has the same personality she had on earth. She also has the same love of flowers, still uses her gift of encouragement, and has the same understanding and knowledge she had when she died. Only now, she is free of her physical health issues, as well as the mental hindrances and deceptions of the sin nature.

Harriet is also growing in wisdom. In heaven Harriet knows to some degree what is happening on earth, just as in the Old Testament the departed Samuel remained aware of Saul's situation on earth. The incident revealing this fact is recounted in 1 Samuel 28:14–19. Israel's King Saul, in trouble and desperately needing counsel, sought out a witch at a place called Endor to act as a medium and call the spirit of Samuel back to earth. When Samuel rose from the grave, he said to Saul:

"Why have you disturbed me by bringing me up?" And Saul answered, "I am greatly distressed; for the Philistines are waging war against me, and God has departed from me and no longer answers me, either through prophets or by dreams; therefore I have called you, that you may make known to me what I should do." (v. 15)

Notice that Saul fully accepted that this apparition was Samuel.

Samuel said, "Why then do you ask me, since the LORD has departed from you and has become your adversary? The LORD has done accordingly as He spoke through me; for the Lord has torn the kingdom out of your hand and given it to your neighbor, to David. As you did not obey the LORD and did not execute His fierce wrath on Amalek, so the LORD has done this thing to you this day." (vv. 16–18)

Samuel was fully aware of what had happened on earth since he died. He acted in his prophetic role and told Saul what would happen next:

Moreover the LORD will also give over Israel along with you into the hands of the Philistines, therefore tomorrow you and your sons will be with me. Indeed the LORD will give over the army of Israel into the hands of the Philistines! (v. 19)

Let me clarify that my point here has nothing to do with the involvement of the medium of Endor, who was certainly a charlatan. The Bible makes it clear that she was stunned that Samuel made an appearance (vv. 12–13). The faker was forced to confront the reality of God. The medium of Endor did not bring Samuel to Saul; instead, God used this communication tool to teach Saul the truth.

This story makes clear the fact that those in heaven are aware of what is happening on earth and are able to communicate with people on earth. It removed any doubt that Harriet was aware of my life and able to communicate with me. God was beginning to teach me this and other truths through my dreams. Harriet is active in heaven, increasing in wisdom, and can see me as God allows. She wants me to know she is well and that God is allowing her communication with me.

Any lingering doubts I might have entertained about the truth of this conclusion were wiped away by accounts of the experiences of others who had lost their mates and encountered similar visitations from them.

C. S. Lewis, who also lost the love of his life, had an unusual dream encounter with his wife, Joy. In his book *A Grief Observed*, he reflected on that dream the morning after it occurred:

> It is often thought that the dead see us. And we assume, whether reasonably or not, that if they see us at all they see us more clearly than before. . . .
>
> It is the quality of last night's experience . . . that makes it worth putting down. It was quite incredibly unemotional. Just the impression of her mind momentarily facing my own. . . . What seemed to meet me was full resolution. Once near the end I said, "If you can—if it is allowed—come to me when I, too, am on my death bed." "Allowed," she said. "Heaven would have a job to hold me; and as for Hell, I'd break it to bits." She knew she was speaking a kind of mythological language, with

an element of comedy in it. There was a twinkle as well as a tear in her eye.[4]

Notice that although Lewis's wife is in heaven, she has full awareness of his earthly desire and even feels his anguish.

In *A Severe Mercy*, Sheldon Vanauken, a close friend of Lewis, also wrote much about his vision of his deceased wife.

It was morning. I had come back to Oxford two years after Davy's death and found digs, . . . I was just dressed to go out to an early lecture at the Schools. Morning sunlight was slanting in the windows. I heard a small sound and turned: it was Davy. I was fully aware that she was dead and, instantly and over-whelmingly, aware that something miraculous was happening. I was, I told myself, full awake.

"Davy!" I cried.

She smiled broadly. I felt pure joy as I took a step towards her, but I also felt a little tentative, hesitant.

"It's all right, dearling," she said, and held out her arms. I went into them, and we hugged each other and kissed—the kiss was heaven. But even in the joy, I was conscious, with a sort of amazement, that she was warm and solid. Weren't ghosts sup-posed to be . . . But I could feel her shoulder blades under my hands. I stood back and looked at her. She looked just as she had always done. . . . I felt an immense gratitude to her, and to God for letting her come. There was, also, just a hint of shy-ness, tentativeness—not knowing quite what the rules were, so to speak, for this sort of thing. I, standing back, looked at her face, her clothes, all in a second or two.

"Davy, Davy!" I said.

"Oh my dear!" she said. Then she added, "I can't stay long."

We went over and sat on the edge of the bed with our arms around each other, and I said something about being grateful for ever that she was there at all. . . .

Then, after a little silence, I said, "Can you tell me one thing, dearling? Are you—well, *with* me sometimes? I've sometimes thought you might be."

"Yes, I am," she said. "I know all your doings."

"Thank God!" I said. Then I said, very casually, "And my letters to you—have you, um, read them? Over my shoulder, maybe?"

She knew—we always knew—that it was important to me. Her arms around me tightened, and she said in a low voice, "Yes, dearling. I've read them all."

And then our eyes met in that look of perfect understanding—that look of *knowing*—that I had missed more than any other thing. After that, we just sat there on the edge of the bed, holding each other, cheek to cheek. There was more said, and there was laughter. And I was pervaded with bliss. I don't recall her exact words, but she gave me to understand that she had wanted this meeting as much as I could have done; and I remember thinking that God had allowed it because He loved her.[5]

In *A Severe Mercy*, Vanauken also stated that Lewis told him he believed God allows departed people to remain close for a period so that we will have the awareness of their reality.[6]

Dallas Willard echoed this conclusion in an interview with Bob Buford, adding, "I do believe that people who have gone on can know what's happening to us, but they're not going to be worried about us because they have a much broader understanding of life than we can begin to imagine."[7]

It was during my readings of Vanauken, Lewis, and Willard that the statement Lewis made about the continued reality of a loved one began to come to fruition for me. At the time, I had been asking God out of my honest grief if Harriet could hear me.

He answered in spectacular and surprising ways that astounded me.

CHAPTER 6

QUESTIONS FOR HEAVEN

Dreams may be one of the most common avenues through which God reaches out to us.

—MORTON KELSEY, *DREAMS: A WAY TO LISTEN TO GOD*

I was at my desk when the phone rang. I picked it up, and the moment I heard Jim's voice, I knew it was one of those calls everyone dreads. "Pete, my doctor just told me the cancer has returned with a vengeance, and he says I have about a month to live. Will you do my funeral?"

I assured him I would, hung up the phone, and headed for the hospital to see him. Just as I arrived, an extraordinary thought entered my mind. I shelved it while I visited with Jim. He was an old friend and a strong believer, and he had no fear of dying. So when we finished discussing his funeral, I asked him about what was on my mind.

"Jim, I have a request for you. I don't get to know many people who are mere days from entering heaven, so I want you to do me a favor. When you get there, would you find Harriet and tell her three things? First, tell her I love her and miss her dearly. Second, tell her I want to know if she can hear me. Third, I don't think she is allowed to answer that question directly, so please ask her to go to Jesus and ask Him to tell me."

He agreed to honor my request and even seemed enthusiastic about doing it. As I drove away from the hospital, I began to wonder if I had done the right thing. A few days later, God in His gracious mercy brought these thoughts to my mind:

Pete, be careful in what you ask. Suppose the answer is yes. Will you be tempted to make Harriet an idol? Will you be tempted to pray to her and not to Me? Will this cause you to be stuck in the past?

I pondered those thoughts in prayer and then replied, *Lord, You know I am capable of letting all three things happen, so if I am seeking to know what is Yours alone, forgive me. Your will be done, not mine. However, please don't hold it against me because I do want to know if it is possible and wise.*

Three days before Jim died, I visited him again. He said, "Pete, I remember those three things you asked me to tell Harriet, and I promise to ask them if possible."

A month passed after his funeral, and nothing happened. I told the Lord if His answer was no, I accepted it.

By this time in my studies of heaven, I had learned two new things. The Bible assures us that we are given spiritual gifts, and Romans 11:29 assures us that our gifts are permanent: "for the gifts and the calling of God are irrevocable." Paul then related our spiritual gifts to being a part of the body of Christ (Romans 12), which further implies their significance and permanence.

In light of these assurances, I was pondering Harriet's gift of encouragement. I also was pondering Revelation 8:3–4, which speaks about how the saints pray in heaven:

Another angel came and stood at the altar, holding a golden censer; and much incense was given to him, so that he might add it to the prayers of all the saints on the golden altar which was before the throne. And the smoke of the incense, with the prayers of the saints, went up before God out of the angel's hand.

It dawned on me that Harriet had prayed for me every day of our earthly life together. So I prayed and asked God if Harriet could remain my prayer partner. If I told Him things to tell her, I knew she would pray for them. I told the Lord I had no reason to believe this could not be true, so if it pleased Him, I would tell Him my prayer requests and ask Him to inform her.

Shortly afterward I received another phone call. This one was from Lisa, a close family friend. "Pete, my sister who has been battling cancer has been given a month to live. Will you do her funeral?"

Though I had met Lisa's sister, I did not know where she was spiritually. She did not attend church, but she had a sharp intellect, which caused her to have a lot of questions about God. I agreed to do the service, but I knew I needed to spend time with her to answer her questions so she could rest in faith in Christ's death for her sins. I prayed for God to help me and asked Him if He would tell Harriet to pray for this precious sister.

Lisa's sister grew into faith in Christ as we met and prayed together. I thanked God for that, and a few weeks later, I conducted her funeral. Two months later, I received a call from Lisa that dramatically loosened grief's tight grip on my heart.

"Pete," she said, "I have struggled so much since my sister died that I have not slept well. Last night I cried myself to sleep. But then the most wonderful thing happened: Harriet came to me in a dream."

As you can imagine, these words caused my heart to leap. "What did she do? What did she say?" I asked.

"I don't remember any words," my friend replied. "I just remember she was encouraging me with her comforting, gentle presence. But she also did a strange thing. She gave me a sheet of yellow lined paper, and it had the word 'Question' written at the top. At the bottom of the page were the words 'Pete Deison.' When I woke up, I was in awe and thanking God. I felt refreshed, encouraged, and loved by God."

For a moment, I just sat there, elated. I knew immediately what the yellow paper meant. I recovered myself and explained it to my friend. "When you told me of your sister's coming death, I asked God if He would make Harriet my prayer partner for her. It appears that in your dream He has answered not only that question but also my question about Harriet being able to hear me."

I wrote this prayer in my journal on July 13, 2013:

Lord, if You are saying to me what I think and hope You are—that Harriet does hear me—would it honor You to corroborate this? According to Your Word, two or more witnesses settle a matter.

🌱

Four days later, I ran into another friend who had recently recovered from serious surgery. Our church family had prayed for her intensely. I told her I was thrilled to see her and glad the surgery was successful.

"Oh, Pete," she replied, "I'm so glad to see you, because there's something I've been needing to tell you. After my surgery, I had a dream about Harriet."

Once again my heart stood still as I eagerly awaited her explanation.

"In the dream, I came to the church to tell the pastors how happy I was that God had answered our prayers. I was not able to find anyone, so I went to the sanctuary. It was empty at first, but then Harriet walked in and said, 'Honey, I will listen. Sit down and tell me all about it.' And I did. I remember glancing at the organ and then to the stained glass and then back to her as I talked. I told her all about the Lord's care over me during my illness and surgery and how I had been spared many awful complications. Harriet just listened, smiling and rejoicing with me. And then, after a pause, I glanced back toward her and she was gone."

After hearing this story, I went home, fell to my knees, and poured out my elation to God. "Lord, You are amazing! I asked for two witnesses to confirm that Harriet does hear me, and You have sent two people—totally unsolicited and unknown to each other— and both have had dreams about Harriet that were directly related to my prayers. Thank You!"

With these corroborations to my experiences, I had reached the point where I had no more room for doubt. Heaven and earth were not closed off from each other, nor were Harriet and I. She was there. She was aware of me and what I was doing. And as God allowed, she was able to communicate to me. My grief instantly lessened. The knowledge that God gave me of my precious wife at work serving Him was amazing proof of His love and gave me great joy.

A BIBLICAL FOUNDATION FOR DREAMS

By this time, my mind was reeling. As a pastor, I base everything on God's Word. It was important for me to know how and where these experiences fit into Scripture. God, of course, was ahead of me. The book I was studying at that time was *Guard Us, Guide Us* by J. I. Packer. In this book, Packer discussed God's guidance and admonishes believers to do seven things in order to find it:

1. Survey the situation, collecting necessary facts.
2. Separate the questions that the situation raises.
3. Search the Scriptures with regard to the situation you are facing.
4. Suspect yourself in relation to the situation.
5. Supplicate (pray) humbly about the situation.
6. Spend unhurried time in deciding how to handle the situation.
7. Submit absolutely to God in relation to the situation.[1]

As I sought to follow Packer's guidance, these thoughts stood out to me. All of life's situations are under God's sovereignty. He knows everything before and after. Also, He plans and decides everything that happens. Finally, He even knows the free-flowing thoughts that run through our minds.

Packer stated, "All the processes of nature are willed and sustained directly by the Creator, every moment, down to the smallest detail, as also are the free-flowing thoughts that run through our minds, *and the dreams that befuddle us while we sleep,* and the self-determined accountable decisions about what we will and will not do that we make in a steady stream throughout our waking hours."[2]

What got my attention was that Packer included dreams in his statement. Not long after I read this, other people, including church elders, pastors, and friends, began seeking me out to tell me about personal experiences of God's grace related to being given dreams about departed loved ones.

One of these dreams—that of a close friend whom I'll call Katy, stands out from the others. When Katy was a child, her older sister died. The two had been extremely close. One night she had a dream in which her sister came to her and said, "It's okay, Katy. I'm okay."

The dream ended and Katy woke up quite upset, crying out to God, "I need more proof than a dream!"

She then went back to sleep and dreamed that her sister returned. She stood by Katy's bed, looked straight at her, and said, "You need more proof? See these books on your nightstand?" Katy watched as with a sweep of her hand, her sister knocked the entire stack of books off the table.

When Katy awoke the next morning, all her books were scattered on the floor. She concluded her story to me, saying, "Seeing those books strewn across the carpet gave me great peace that my sister really communicated to me in that dream and that her continued existence is a reality."

With Packer's guidelines for seeking God's direction firmly planted in my mind, I began an intense search of Scripture and the writings of respected theologians to gain a deeper understanding of dreams. It was clear to me from the beginning that dreams had always been one of God's communication channels to humans. As Dallas Willard said in his book *Hearing God*, "God addresses us in various ways: in dreams, visions and voices; through the Bible and extraordinary events; and so forth."[3] I was already beginning to learn the truth of this observation through experience, so my next step was to continue my search to be sure I was standing on a strong scriptural foundation.

When Heaven Lets Down the Ladder

Through methodical study, I learned that the Scriptures are filled with dreams. Jacob had the first full and significant dream recorded in the Bible, and as the first dream, it has seminal importance. God was setting a precedent, so its details carry great weight.

> Then Jacob departed from Beersheba and went toward Haran. He came to a certain place and spent the night there, because the sun had set; and he took one of the stones of the place and put it under his head, and lay down in that place. He had a dream, and behold, a ladder was set on the earth with its top reaching to heaven; and behold, the angels of God were ascending and descending on it. (Genesis 28:10–12)

Note the details of the dream, especially the connection between earth and heaven.

> And behold, the LORD stood above it and said, "I am the LORD, the God of your father Abraham and the God of Isaac; the land on which you lie, I will give it to you and to your descendants. Your descendants will also be like the dust of the earth, and you

will spread out to the west and to the east and to the north and to the south; and in you and in your descendants shall all the families of the earth be blessed. (vv. 13–14)

In this section, God restated His covenant with Abraham and his descendants:

"Behold, I am with you and will keep you wherever you go, and will bring you back to this land; for I will not leave you until I have done what I have promised you." Then Jacob awoke from his sleep and said, "Surely the LORD is in this place, and I did not know it." He was afraid and said, "How awesome is this place! This is none other than the house of God, and this is the gate of heaven." (vv. 15–17)

In this Scripture passage, Jacob dreamed of a ladder set up on earth and reaching heaven. Angels of God were ascending and descending on it. The Lord stood above and restated His covenant and commitment to protect Jacob and return him to the land where He was developing His plan for His people. When Jacob awoke, he declared the place to be the house of God and the gate of heaven.

Several things are important about this first dream:

1. God provided a connection between Himself and earth.
2. He had messengers going back and forth (Hebrews 1:14).
3. He was focused on His covenant plan and His covenant people and, at this point, His care for His human agent, Jacob.
4. God used a dream to convey this.
5. Jacob called the place the gate to heaven.

Throughout the Bible, we read of God communicating with people in many different ways. He spoke to Moses through a burning bush, to Abraham through an angel, to many people through prophets, and once even through a donkey! God, in His boundless creativity, seems willing to use any means that is effective to get His message across. And beginning here with His communication to Jacob, we find God speaking in dreams many times throughout the Bible both to His people and unbelievers alike.

Job 33:14–15 reminds us that dreams are one of the creative forms of communication God uses to fulfill His purposes: "Indeed God speaks once, or twice, yet no one notices it. In a dream, a vision of the night, when sound sleep falls on men, while they slumber in their beds."

Several chapters after the account of Jacob's dream in Genesis, we find Joseph interpreting Pharaoh's dreams:

> Pharaoh said to Joseph, "I have had a dream, but no one can interpret it; and I have heard it said about you, that when you hear a dream you can interpret it." Joseph then answered Pharaoh, saying, "It is not in me; God will give Pharaoh a favorable answer." (Genesis 41:15–16)

Notice that although the dream is given to Pharaoh in symbols, God stands by ready to make it understandable.

Daniel had several highly significant dreams and interpreted the prophetic dreams God sent to Nebuchadnezzar.

> Daniel answered before the king and said, "As for the mystery about which the king has inquired, neither wise men, conjurers,

magicians nor diviners are able to declare it to the king. However, there is a God in heaven who reveals mysteries, and He has made known to King Nebuchadnezzar what will take place in the latter days. This was your dream and the visions in your mind while on your bed. As for you, O king, while on your bed your thoughts turned to what would take place in the future; and He who reveals mysteries has made known to you what will take place. But as for me, this mystery has not been revealed to me for any wisdom residing in me more than in any other living man, but for the purpose of making the interpretation known to the king, and that you may understand the thoughts of your mind." (Daniel 2:27–30)

In a dream, the wise men, after visiting Jesus, received a warning from God that they should not return to Herod:

And having been warned by God in a dream not to return to Herod, the magi left for their own country by another way. (Matthew 2:12)

Joseph received a dream warning him that King Herod was seeking to kill Jesus, which enabled him to escape to Egypt with his family:

Now when they had gone, behold, an angel of the Lord appeared to Joseph in a dream and said, "Get up! Take the Child and His mother and flee to Egypt, and remain there until I tell you; for Herod is going to search for the Child to destroy Him." (Matthew 2:13)

In the New Testament, God gave various visions to Peter, Paul, and John:

> . . . and he saw the sky opened up, and an object like a great sheet coming down, lowered by four corners to the ground. (Acts 10:11)

> *A vision appeared to Paul in the night*: a man of Macedonia was standing and appealing to him, and saying, "Come over to Macedonia and help us." When he had seen the vision, immediately we sought to go into Macedonia, concluding that God had called us to preach the gospel to them. (Acts 16:9–10)

Communicative dreams such as these were not merely phenomena of Bible times. God clearly intended for them to continue into the future. In explaining the coming of the Holy Spirit, the sign of the new covenant, Peter said, "Your young men shall see visions, and your old men shall dream dreams" (Acts 2:17).

My study of Scripture helped me understand that God uses dreams as one of His creative communication tools to fulfill His purposes, not just in the past but also in the present. I now knew that in coming to this conclusion, I was standing on solid, biblical ground—and I was not standing alone.

DREAMS IN THE EARLY CHURCH

The early church fathers commonly considered dreams to be a means of communication from God. Polycarp, a friend of the apostle John, wrote of a dream he had in which he died a martyr's death in Rome. That dream later became a reality. Irenaeus believed that dreams were "a means for him to maintain a proper contact with God." Origen discussed dreams in several of his books, as did Clement, another early church father. Tertullian believed dreams were extremely important and wrote extensively of them in his book *The Anima*. He did not mince words in expressing his conviction on the subject: "Is it not known to all the people that the dream is the most usual way that God reveals himself to man?"[4]

During the time period when the doctrinal creeds of the church were being established, Athanasius and his contemporary church fathers valued dreams. Other church fathers following them also wrote extensively about dreams, including Jerome, Gregory the Great, Bernard of Clairvaux, and Francis of Assisi.

And even in the present day, well-known author Eric Metaxas gave his testimony in the June 2013 issue of *Christianity Today*. He related a dream in which God spoke to him and left him with a feeling of "new and newness." When he was asked what the dream meant, his reply surprised even himself:

> I said what I never would have said before—and would have cringed to hear anyone else say. I said that I had accepted Jesus. And when I spoke those words, I was flooded with the same joy I had had inside the dream. And I've had that joy with me for the past 25 years.[5]

All of this history of God communicating through dreams—in the Bible, in the early church, and in the present—boils down to the sovereignty of God. Dreams are His realm, not ours. He is the initiator; we are the recipients. He obviously uses dreams, but He does so in His wisdom and for His purposes.

The Bible is God's primary means of communicating to us, and it is the sole means of conveying theological truth. It is the foundation upon which we interpret and discern our lives. Understand this: no dream that contradicts Scripture is from God. I want to ensure that this perspective is in place throughout all I write in this book. I do not take dreams as guidance or information without first going to Scripture. I see all dreams through the lens of personalized grace. My dreams were experiences God gave me—and is still giving me. The dreams are gifts of His grace, not commands or directions.

I had asked God for confirmation of Harriet's presence in heaven, and for reasons only He knows, He allowed it. This was His choice and not mine. I just knew I was grateful.

CHAPTER 7

GIFTS OF GRACE—
MORE DREAMS

I will bless the LORD who has counseled me;
Indeed, my mind instructs me in the night.

—PSALM 16:7

At this point in my journey through grief, I had received from God three remarkable dreams of Harriet, and two friends had reported to me their dreams of her in which she had used her gift of encouragement to help them through difficult times. In addition, I had done an extensive study on dreams, searching the Scriptures, history, and the recorded experiences of respected believers. This study had confirmed to me the reality of what my friends and I had experienced.

As far as I knew, however, the dreams were over. They had served their purpose in giving me God's assurance of Harriet's reality, answering the questions pressing on my spirit, and greatly reducing the intensity of my grief. I had been greatly blessed, both by the dreams and by my study of Scripture, and I realized that through it all I had gained insights and understanding I had never had before.

It occurred to me that these insights might benefit others who were burdened with grief. It would not be right for me to hoard to myself all I had learned and experienced; I knew I had to share this remarkable display of God's grace. As I shared my experiences, I was asked repeatedly if I would write about them. So I prayed, *Lord, I would be blessed and happy for the rest of my life with the two dreams others had about Harriet. They have taken away much of my grief. If You want me to write about this and if it would honor You, may I be so bold as to ask You to give me however many more dreams you determine are wise?*

God's answer to that prayer exceeded anything I could have imagined. Within a few months of praying, five more people came to tell me they had had dreams about Harriet. And dreams of her began to flow one after the other directly to me. In fact, since I began to write this book, I have received more than one hundred dreams of Harriet, not all as significant as others, yet no less real. I have recorded them all, and I thank God for every one of them. They encouraged me deeply and, coming as they did in answer to a specific prayer, confirmed that I should indeed share my story.

Dreams of Harriet's Friends and Family

The dreams of Harriet reported to me by her friends and our family varied in significance. Some were short and enigmatic, containing statements or acts that aroused curiosity or a need for explanation. Others were clear, encouraging, and even light and cheery.

For example, about a month after Harriet's death, she appeared in a dream to one of her close friends. The friend told me that when she saw Harriet in the dream, she asked, "Is everything they say about heaven really true?"

"Yes," replied Harriet, smiling and giggling as she spoke. It was as if heaven was far more delightful and grand than she could convey.

Another friend told me about a dream in which she saw Harriet deep in thought. The only thing she said was, "I should have loved my family differently." She offered no explanation for the statement, but whatever it meant, she was pondering this thought yet not distraught.

A dream less enigmatic and probably more significant came from a friend of Harriet's who shares her birthday and also suffers from depression.

"Since Harriet died," the friend told me, "I often sense her presence. She also comes to me in my dreams, where she seems to be standing like a sentinel, guarding my heart and thoughts. It goes like this: When anxiety and depression break through, suicide pops into my mind, and sometimes I say the word out loud. Harriet then calmly and smilingly whispers 'no' and redirects my thoughts. I can't tell you how comforting and soothing this is. I have been fighting depression for years. Harriet is so helpful and has been since, it seems, almost from the instant she died."

A friend who was part of a women's Bible study that Harriet cotaught shared a dream she had about her on the day of Harriet's funeral. She wrote in her journal,

I think in my dream I was setting up for an event and saw Harriet over to the side, sitting. I went and asked if she had told anyone she was considering taking her life before she did it, and she said, "No." I said, "Oh, Harriet," and cried. She looked beautiful and had her smile back. At some point, she said she was "giving me her Purpose." Apparently, when a person died, they could do that.

The next day Harriet's friend wrote, "Last night, before the dream, I had been depressed and feeling useless. The bible verse that came to me two or three times after the dream was, 'I came to give you life, and life more abundantly.'" She told me, "That is when I connected the dream. Purpose must have meant abundant life."

The two most informative and surprising dreams have come from my family members. My younger daughter, Ann, told me she had not had dreams like those I was having. I told her that I would pray for her. A month later she called me early one morning and said, "I just had the most wonderful dream about Mom." She described the dream as one filled with loving encouragement.

"But," she continued, "before the dream was finished, my son came into the room and woke me up. I shooed him into the kitchen to get breakfast and tried hard to go back to sleep, hoping Mom would come back and finish the dream. But I was too distressed to get back to sleep. I began to sob and cry out, 'Mother, please don't leave!' In a moment the dream returned, and Mom told me, 'It's okay; you don't need me anymore, and besides, I do not control when I can come!'"

Those concluding words sent chills up my spine. I said, "Do you realize how important that statement is? That means every dream I've had about your mom has occurred because God allowed it. She wants to come, but she does so only when God determines it is best or wise. Wow! Every dream I've had of her has been a gift from God." I wept and thanked God.

One of the most comforting yet mysterious dreams of Harriet came through my granddaughter, who was eight at the time. She related the dream to her mother, who e-mailed it to me.

I had a dream last night where I walked out of my room and into your house. I walked into your room and saw Mumsie [her grandmother name for Harriet] sitting there.

"Hi, Mumsie!" I called out.

She held out her arms toward me and said, "Come here, sweetie."

I climbed into her lap. We laughed and talked and then she said, "Shhhh" and pointed to you, Grandy. You were praying for her. She told me that she likes to watch you pray for her. So Mumsie and I watched you pray for a while, and then I woke up.

This dream both thrilled me and troubled me for days. I didn't know how to process the fact that Harriet was watching me pray for her. Private prayers are seldom if ever like those you hear led publicly in church. They are more informal and conversational, and they issue forth in a stream-of-consciousness flow. The idea of Harriet watching me pray made me feel a little self-conscious about the process. If I was onstage, so to speak, maybe I should polish my prayers a bit, think them through beforehand.

But my granddaughter's words seemed to counter this idea: "She *likes* to watch you pray for her." Obviously Harriet found joy in watching me pray. That convinced me to continue my prayers "warts and all," just as I had always rendered them.

My New Stream of Dreams

As my dreams of Harriet continue to flow, I have been diligent to record every one of them. In trying to understand them better, I group them into four categories: encouragement, information, romance, and fear.

Dreams offering encouragement are the most frequent, which isn't surprising, because encouragement is Harriet's spiritual gift. These dreams encourage me by providing assurance of Harriet's happiness, activity, laughter, and love. In many of these dreams, I tell Harriet I miss her, and she replies, "I know." Then she always adds, "I love you, Pete." In such dreams, Harriet and I have danced, dined, attended solemn ceremonies, and simply talked about daily life.

The informative dreams teach me something. One of Harriet's lessons, which I mentioned earlier, was that I needed to get on with my life. In one dream, I told her she is beautiful, and she replied—confidently yet comfortably—"I know it." There was no pride or arrogance in the assertion. She was merely affirming an obvious fact: God had given her beauty. It was His doing, not hers.

It surprised me to learn that in heaven Harriet often goes to meetings and gives her testimony. Maybe someday I will learn whom she meets with and understand the purpose of these meetings. Early in the summer of 2014, Harriet told me in a dream that she was busy but would come later. From this I learned that she has duties and schedules in heaven. In another dream, I told her I had a hard time looking at her pictures, and she simply said, "Then don't look at them." Simple enough. Heaven's wisdom seems to be similar to earthly logic. In one dream, I said to Harriet, "My dreams are so real. Are you really in them?" She replied, "Yes, and I recall them just as you do, and we discuss what to do with them."

I have no idea what she meant or who is included in the "we" who discusses the dreams. However, it comforts me to know that the dreams are as important to her and to heaven as they are to me.

Then there are the romantic dreams, many of which are frankly very physical. In these dreams, the Lord reminds me that marital intimacy points to our desire for communion or connection with Him at our deepest level. Marital intimacy has always symbolized something spiritual. In his book *Everything Belongs*, Richard Rohr spoke of this mystery:

> Often the imagery becomes sexual, because it is the only adequate language to describe this contemplative experience. I have often wondered why God would give his creatures such a strong and constant fascination with another's image, form, and face. Why would God take such a risk unless it were an important risk? What is the connection between our human passion and knowing God? Are all relationships a school of communion?[1]

The final category of my dreams is fear. These fear-based dreams are the rarest, but they are the most disturbing. They express my fear of losing Harriet. She is as present in these dreams as in the others, but when I reach out to her or speak to her, she does not respond. It's as if she is unaware of me or unconcerned about me.

These fear-based dreams are the hardest for me to accept. Their meaning is clear: they are a product of grief. Harriet has left this present physical life, yet my heart still craves her presence. When I cannot find her in my dreams, the sense of disconnection causes pain and fear. Will all my dreams cease at some point, severing my connection with her altogether? How will I live with that frightening possibility? This dilemma is, no doubt, the underlying cause of my fear-based dreams.

I never know when the dreams will come. Sometimes there are weeks or months between them, and at other times they follow each other in a rapid torrent. I often wonder if they will cease. If a time comes when God chooses to withhold the dreams because I no longer need them, then I will be content and secure in the knowledge that He is sufficient for all my needs and well-being. Meanwhile, I thank Him for the wonderful gifts He gives me.

THE AFFIRMATION OF DREAMS

The dreams God has given me about Harriet and heaven speak of the reality of life to come: the reality that our lives continue after death. They affirm that we retain our personalities and memories in heaven and that those on the other side of the veil know us, love us, and pray for us. They are eager to reconnect with us. As cartoonist Bill Watterson's Hobbes once told Calvin, "I think we dream so we don't have to be apart so long. If we are in each other's dreams, we can be together all the time."[2]

It is important to remember that dreams are only one tool God uses to show grace. And for balance, the Scriptures warn us that not all dreams have a divine origin. Ecclesiastes 5:7 speaks to this point: "For in many dreams and in many words there is emptiness. Rather, fear God."

Yet there can be no doubt that many dreams do have a divine origin. Shortly after leading Israel out of Egypt, God told Moses, Aaron, and Miriam, "If there is a prophet among you, I, the LORD, shall make Myself known to him in a vision. I shall speak with him in a dream" (Numbers 12:6).

Do I believe all my dreams about Harriet are directly from God, or is it possible that they are just created from my memories and longings? I have two answers to this question, both of which affirm that my dreams are indeed from God. First, if I were the only one who had received dreams of Harriet, I might be hesitant to claim that they were objective realities. But since others have also dreamed of her and received information from her, as well as the specific answers to my prayer request, I am certain that the dreams are from God. Second, these dreams could not have been concocted randomly in my subconscious from my own memories, because so many of them reveal new information that I did not have in memory.

I love the work of George MacDonald, who wrote:

> Such a dream must have yet lovelier truth at the heart of its dreaming!
>
> In moments of doubt, I cry, "Could God Himself create such lovely things as I dreamed?"
>
> "Whence then came thy dream?" answers Hope. . . .
>
> When a man dreams his own dream, he is the sport [center] of his dream; when Another gives it to him, that Other is able to fulfill it.[3]

These facts, along with my extensive study of dreams, convince me that my dreams come from the sovereign God who loves and encourages us. Thus I accept them fully as gifts given by His hand.

Should every person with a need seek answers from God through dreams? Not necessarily. Of course, we should all seek God's wisdom and grace first from Scripture, but we should be open to whatever way He chooses to minister to us. Just because

He communicated with me through dreams does not mean that is the way He will choose for you. Yes, He has spoken to His people throughout history through dreams, but He has also spoken in many other ways. His grace is varied and personal.

God treats each individual with uniqueness because He crafted each of us to reflect some unique aspect of His glory. As the apostle Paul wrote, "For we are His workmanship, created in Christ Jesus for good works, which God prepared beforehand so that we would walk in them" (Ephesians 2:10). He created you with some ability or purpose that no one else on the planet shares. Therefore, He will communicate with you in ways that best fit your own uniqueness. And when you are able to rest and trust Him in this, you too will find great comfort and even blessing.

Always begin with the Scripture and then wait upon Him to bring His thoughts to you. Paul told us the Holy Spirit combines spiritual thoughts with spiritual words (the Bible). Read and think, read and pray! He will speak.

CHAPTER 8

THE LANDSCAPE OF GRIEF

You cannot jettison grief
For it is solid and heavy
A stone building block.
But look! It has become
The cornerstone, the foundation
On which is built
What you are to become.

—ANNE COKE

As I look back on the years since Harriet took her life, only now can I wipe the fog off my glasses and focus clearly on the landscape of grief. I have come to accept the hard truth that we cannot understand most of life until we have lived it. John Claypool grasped this fact when he wrote, "If insight comes at all, it will not be before, but only through and after experience."[1]

On my journey of grief, insight has jumped out in multiple moments, much like billboards seen whizzing by from a speeding train. Now, years after Harriet's death as I assemble these billboard thoughts, I realize that there is no logical progression for grief. It does not move in a linear direction. It has no boundaries; it floods every fiber of the soul. It has no standards, so you never know where you stand in its obscure path. You think you have progressed to a certain point only to find yourself back on ground you have trod before.

Yet there are some common impacts and circumstances that every grieving person faces, such as what to do with the departed person's possessions, how to respond to attempted comfort from people who mean well but don't do it well, handling holidays, and so forth. But even these common occurrences are individualized. Every loss has unique needs and circumstances.

So the pages that follow paint a picture rather than plot a pathway through grief. The landscape of grief is filled with multiple trails and signposts. But the rules of traversing this landscape do not follow the normal logic of place and time. If you are like me, you may not be able to detect a clear movement from one stage to the next, even though you will progress through those stages.

Traversing the landscape of grief is not a journey of choice; it's one that is forced on you. But it is full of purpose. Be warned, however, that grief never leaves you; it carves into your soul a permanent scar. The pain lessens, yet the sensitivity to the scar always remains. But the journey is necessary and full of purpose. Undertake it and you become able to resume your life and again experience happiness and joy.

The Desert

The first part of grief is a plunge into darkness. The tragic loss occurs, and nothing is clear to you anymore. You feel as if you are walking through the desert at night. It seems as if nothing is there—and this is because nothing seems to matter anymore. All you can see is what is not there.

In the days and weeks following Harriet's death, I walked in this desert darkness with no idea where my next footstep would land. There was no light, and the terrain was horribly uneven. But I didn't care. Nothing really mattered. I did only what I had to do, what I was required to do. I wrote in my journal, "Life feels so forced."

There were tender moments of help from friends who cared. I soaked these moments into my parched heart like water, but the pitch-black darkness remained—until I met someone who shared my circumstance. She, too, had been blindsided by a loved one's suicide. She reached out, took my hand, and said, "I understand. Walk over here; it's a little smoother." She knew my anguish; she could finish my sentences. I grabbed her hand like a lost little boy and did not want to let go.

But because she was farther along than I on the path of grief, she could only take me so far. I wept when she left, but later I realized she was right. I had to learn to walk by myself.

Although my fellow traveler helped a little, I was still in the desert. I could better see the landscape, but nothing looked pleasant. None of the old joys soothed me—not my work, not the cabin, not reading, not my church. The hole was so deep and the pain so great that I could not even fully appreciate family or friends. But they were patient, and though I could not tell it, God was working on me behind the scenes. This was a terribly dry time.

THE FLATLANDS

My slog through the desert sand, which kept my eyes looking downward to find footing, slowly gave way to the firmer flatlands. While the ground may have felt more solid under my feet, the landscape was still bleak and featureless. But at least I could now walk rather than shuffle and stumble, and I was able to look forward rather than down. I began to acknowledge that God was indeed in control, and He provided what I needed daily to carry on. It was while I was in the flatlands that God began to give me dreams about Harriet and other gifts of grace that I could not ignore.

Harriet's death had not robbed me of the hope of heaven because I knew that death was not final. It was a doorway to a new, full-of-life, exciting world for Harriet. I thrived on this knowledge for many months, yet my life was still a daily walk in the flatlands of duty, plodding ever forward, one foot in front of the other. I could look up and realize there was life ahead, but I could not get excited about it. I woke up daily and didn't want to live. I didn't want to die; I just didn't want to live without Harriet. The flatlands looked the same in every direction. Nothing was inviting. I didn't want to initiate anything or make plans.

It was during this stage that my friends really helped. God was at work in them, and I appreciated their attempts to help me—but as I now realize, not as much as I should have. I had reached a point where life seemed so bleak that I didn't want anything—not even help. But they persisted and kept an anticipation of a new future in front of me.

One of these boosts from friends came on an afternoon when I was unusually lonely and depressed. For me, afternoons are the hardest time of day. It is then that my brain feels its addiction to connecting with Harriet. On this particular afternoon, the gloom was so deep that I asked God for help. Almost instantly my phone rang.

"Pete, this is Frank," boomed the voice on the line. "I'm out in front of your house. Let's go get some nachos and beer."

I'm not a big beer drinker, but I wasn't going to pass up the gift of fun and love that Frank was offering. We had a blast. Friends like Frank and my family members carried me through most of the flatlands when life seemed so dull. I knew it was God's goodness working through them, and their care was invaluable to me at this stage of my grief.

If the desert forced me to cling to God and His Word, the flatlands gave me the gift of time. My church leadership told me to work as little or as much as I wanted. Grief was giving me something I didn't even realize I desperately needed: time to read and study. Along with the Bible, I read many of the books in Harriet's library. Doing so gave me the gift of gratitude. This was a huge boost to the healing of my pain.

Until you truly value the past, you will never have a vision for a future. One phrase I remembered reading in one of Harriet's books stuck in my mind at this point: "Every exit is also an entrance. You never walk out of one thing without walking into something else."[2] This truth propelled me to study voraciously about heaven, Harriet's new home. I began to get excited about her new life, and slowly the landscape began to change once more.

THE FOOTHILLS

One day I looked up and found that the terrain of grief wasn't as dull and lifeless as it had been. My pain was still there; I was reminded of it daily. But because of the dreams, I was more aware of Harriet's new life in heaven. This awareness allowed me to lift up my eyes from the ground and the bleak landscape I was emerging from to the hills in front of me.

The downside to this was that I was also more aware of Harriet's absence on earth. Every day grief made me aware of what

I was missing as I watched couples hold hands, listened to love songs, and saw romantic scenes in movies. I observed the joy in my married friends that I had once taken for granted.

This acute awareness made my life a roller coaster of continual ups and downs. Yet God was still giving me strength for the journey. Death was an exit for Harriet, but it was also an entrance into something new for me. I began to see Harriet's life as a gift of God's love specifically suited to and tailored for me. I also began to see her death as a gift for her because my recent experiences and revelations enabled me to view heaven in a new, exciting way. At the same time, God was showing me that, as painful as Harriet's death is for me, He still intends me good. Somehow Harriet's death was intended for my good.

God does not always give us whatever we want, but He always has our best in mind. This has always been His promise. "God causes all things to work together for good to those who love God, to those who are called according to His purpose" (Romans 8:28). Note the key parts of this verse:

1. "Work together"—This implies a process. The hoped-for result is not instantaneous.
2. "For good"—This is God's ultimate goal for us.
3. "To those who love God"—I can see God's good only if I choose to love Him.
4. "Called according to His purpose"—He has a purpose for my life that holds firm even in the most difficult circumstances.

God's grace is sufficient, but it is not an anesthetic. My struggle was diminishing but not ending. I had reached the foothills, and my grief was leading me higher yet. The upward climb had begun, and I sensed some highly desirable goal drawing me on. That goal, as I soon learned, was the coming acceptance of my new reality.

THE MOUNTAINS

From the foothills, the elevation increases and you reach the mountains that loom high above them. The steepness of the climb forces you to make harder decisions. My first decision was the choice that I wanted to go on in the climb. I would persevere. God in His grace had been carrying me along with continuous blessings. I had to come to terms with the truth that grief has a purpose. The wisdom of Denver Seminary professor Dr. James Means helped solidify this truth for me:

> Each agonizing moment is essential or God would not allow it. To be counted worthy of suffering is to enter an entirely new realm of spiritual experience. My suffering is seen as instrumental, not accidental, to the purposes of a loving God.[3]

As hard as it is to fully grasp, God created grief. I don't mean that grief was part of His original perfect creation, but given the tragic and devastating effects of the Fall, He inserted it into creation somewhat like a physician prescribes an antidote. God gave us grief to help us counter the effects of death—to keep it from overcoming us completely. Grief acts as a shield that protects us during the final stages of loss. I had to grasp that God is just as much in control of my grief journey as He was of Harriet's death. So rather than try to escape from grief, I needed to see it through, to learn from it. This was a hard climb. I knew I would never fully understand Harriet's death this side of heaven, but I could use the strain and exertion of the ascent through grief to grow steadily stronger.

It was during this higher climb that my focus shifted. Throughout the earlier stages of the landscape, grief had kept me extremely self-centered. Yet by acknowledging this fact and confessing it to God, He began to show me that I wasn't alone.

One night my friend Rick invited me to dinner with two other men. Stephen had lost his wife, Joyce, a close friend of Harriet's, a year before. I had not reached out to him. Rob had just placed his wife in a full-care Alzheimer's unit. She was still alive, but their life together had died.

This encounter with fellow sufferers showed me that my grief was not singular. It was the common lot of humans living in a fallen world. There was no need for me to enclose myself in a cocoon as if I were the only one suffering loss. I needed to get out of myself. I needed to accept the fact that loss does not define me. What defines me is how I respond to that loss. Jerry Sittser once said, "It is not what happens *to* us that matters as much as what happens *in* us."[4]

It was another turning point for me. I chose to look at my life to determine what I had left and what new I could gain. I continued to climb, finding new footholds and ledges to grip as I made my way upward until I eventually reached the peak. From there I could see my grief differently. The mountains taught me that grief has a purpose, but the view from those peaks showed me I had a long way to come down. At the summit, I felt better, but I was also confused because from my new vantage point, I encountered a lot of options.

THE FOREST

Coming down from a mountain, you find yourself facing a timberline. When you enter a forest, you smell fresh scents, you hear new sounds, and you see large trees that seem to have no order. There are no trails; at least none are clearly marked. Which direction should you go?

As I entered the forest, I felt small. Yet I felt a sense of expectation. I sensed that I had walked through the worst of grief and something better lay ahead.

When my grief began to lessen, it surprised me to find that what I felt was not relief; it was loneliness. Apparently my grief had become a companion of sorts, and painful though it was, it filled the empty space left by Harriet's absence. The forest made me acutely aware of how alone I was. My prayers began to search for ways to cover this feeling. But then God reminded me that there is a difference between being lonely and being alone. Loneliness made me look inward and feel like a victim. Being alone made me aware that I am an individual of worth, and that I have abilities and the capacity to move forward. Even more important, I realized that God created me and He is always with me. Hebrews 13:5 became my compass verse: "I will never desert you, nor will I ever forsake you." I was picking my way through the trees by myself, but I was being guided by an ever-present God.

Even though I was filled with confusion and doubt, which are acute aspects of grief, I had to choose a direction through the uncharted maze and begin walking. My brain rattled the questions: *What am I supposed to do with my life now? What is my new normal?* The idea of "new normal" didn't sound fun. I did a lot of waiting. And then I waited some more.

In time God brought me to a place of emptiness, but this, too, had a purpose. I was waiting for a new fullness. I wanted to know what God had in store for me. It is extremely hard to wait during grief. My journey had led me to a place where I could see God at work, but the timing was not under my control. I was waiting, but this did not mean I was passive.

Waiting is like the planting cycle. I knew God was at work in my life. And even though it took time to see that work, I sought Him daily and faithfully fulfilled my normal, everyday responsibilities. These actions were like adding fertilizer to the seeds of His next direction for my life. In his book *God Is in the Manger*, Dietrich Bonhoeffer summed it up this way: "Waiting is an art. . . . It happens . . . according to the divine laws of sprouting, growing, and becoming."[5]

I love the way Eugene Peterson rephrased Romans 8:24–25 in *The Message*: "Waiting does not diminish us, any more than waiting diminishes a pregnant mother. We are enlarged in the waiting. We, of course, don't see what is enlarging us. But the longer we wait, the larger we become, and the more joyful our expectancy." As I waited, I often needed to be reminded of Jeremiah's words to the Israelites going into exile, which was certainly a grief-filled event: "'I know the plans that I have for you,' declares the LORD, 'plans for welfare and not for calamity to give you a future and a hope'" (Jeremiah 29:11).

In Michael O'Brien's novel *Sophia House*, the main character, Pawel, has an imagined conversation with God. He tells God his deepest feelings and then demands that God speak to him. Here is the dialogue O'Brien presented:

"I am alone," he seethed. "Why am I alone?"

You feel alone, my son.

"Am I a son? I do not feel like a son."

You are a son.

The bitterness swelled into vehemence. "I have no father!" he cried angrily.

You have a father.

"Where is my father? The place where he should be is empty."

Emptiness is a place of waiting.

"I have waited all my life."

A little longer and you will be full.

"I will wait and no one will come."

All is coming to you.

"I do not believe it. Happiness is for others. Not for me."

Those who think they are full cannot receive. You can receive.

"I am filling, filling, filling—with pain. That is all, just pain."

After a long emptiness, the filling is felt as pain.[6]

When we are waiting, O'Brien reminds us, God is there to fill us once we are empty. Jesus said a seed cannot bear fruit unless it falls into the ground and dies (John 12:24). When I was in the forest, it hit me that some things needed to die in my life before I was empty:

- The discontent of singleness
- Procrastination of action, waiting for others to fill me
- Fear of the unknown
- Joylessness

This emptying was like emotional rehab. It meant letting God have all my fears. The person I had been with Harriet was irretrievable, but once I rested that fact with God, the person I could become was a great story yet to be revealed. As I weaved my way through the trees, God gave me more confidence and anticipation concerning what was to come. When I told Him I was afraid of letting Harriet go, He reminded me that I wasn't giving her up; I was giving her over to His care.

There are great possibilities in the forest. Each path I faced meant making a new decision, and each new decision drew me closer to the gift God had waiting for me. My decision to let go of the past helped me find new paths that had not been visible before. I knew this to be true when I decided to make plans for the future. Plans to go fishing. Plans to take my family places. Plans to take a group from my church to Israel. I admit I did these things with less enthusiasm than in the past, but the closer the time for each event came, the more my anticipation grew. Decisive activity is positive therapy.

The forest is scary, and some of the paths are formidable. But my growing sense of anticipation gave me a sense of direction and made my steps more secure. It is easy to get lost in the forest. There are so many trails that go nowhere, but I trusted that God would guide me.

Even though I walk through the valley of the shadow of death, I fear no evil, for You are with me; Your rod and Your staff, they comfort me. (Psalm 23:4)

The Meadows

Finally, I emerged from the forest into the meadows. That is where I am now. Meadows are places of greater joy. New beauty begins to appear in the landscape of grief. I don't mean continuous sunlight and flowers. The forest gives way to small meadows at first. Here I've found patches of unbroken sunlight and swaths of wildflowers that bring increasing moments of happiness. The forest still surrounds me, yet these open spaces continue to be doors of surprise.

Harriet's life and death have blessed many people. The letters I have received have filled me with meadow-like joy. My open honesty about my sufferings has brought hope to many people in the midst of their own grief. My knowledge of heaven has encouraged many suffering and dying people. My new voice enables me to speak deeply at funerals and lift up my own painful moments to inspire hope in others. All of these blessings are bright spots that feel like sunlit meadows.

Living in the meadows, however, sometimes scares me, because there is much joy and freedom here. It is a new, unknown freedom, one without Harriet. The thought *Can I really enjoy this?* often creeps into my mind, as if there were something dishonoring about allowing myself to be happy without her.

Grief has an odd, warm, womb-like feel akin to a security blanket, yet it becomes confining as you grow. God wants us to be free from such self-imposed boundaries. He wants us to run joyfully through the meadows He provides. The apostle Paul wrote, "It was for freedom that Christ set us free" (Galatians 5:1). God wants us to choose love, to love others, and to love again. To love is to find joy.

In his book *A Grace Disguised*, Jerry Sittser framed the challenge of this freedom:

> The problem of choosing to love again is that the choice to love
> means living under the constant threat of future loss. But the

problem of choosing not to love is that the choice to turn from love means imperiling the life of the soul, for the soul thrives in an environment of love. Soul-full people love; soul-less people do not. If people want their souls to grow through loss, whatever the loss is, they must eventually decide to love even more deeply than they did before.[7]

THE PICTURE AS A WHOLE

I am still traveling in the landscape of grief because there is no straight and unbroken path through it. Pain can pop up at any moment. But here is the difference: I can now see the whole picture. I have a bird's-eye view of the landscape. I can look at each phase of my grief journey and know that every part of it has a purpose and a reason. And when I can compare the whole to the momentary parts of grief that I have endured and occasionally still visit me, I grasp what Paul meant when he said:

> Therefore we do not lose heart, but though our outer man is decaying, yet our inner man is being renewed day by day. For momentary, light affliction is producing for us an eternal weight of glory far beyond all comparison, while we look not at the things which are seen, but at the things which are not seen; for the things which are seen are temporal, but the things which are not seen are eternal. (2 Corinthians 4:16–18)

I would like to share twelve lessons I have learned that made grief more bearable for me. They are my fellow-struggler counsel for you.

1. Tell God everything—good, bad, scary, and ugly. He gave me perspective about it all. This is the value of prayer.

2. Write things out to help vague thoughts and feelings become clear, because grief creates a lot of vagueness. Keep a journal. This guides you toward clarity.

3. Accept that grief has a purpose. I became more relaxed in the process when I reached this landmark. This creates hope.

4. Know that grief is not permanent. God still has a plan for your happiness. This provides perspective.

5. Help people help you by telling them what to pray for. You won't always know how you feel or what you need, and it's okay to admit that! This is honesty.

6. Scriptures are healing for the soul. Read them daily. God's words are the best words. This creates strength.

7. Reflect on the time you had with the one you lost and thank God for all that person did for you. It helps you let go. Confess your failings and review your loved one's failings as well. This is cleansing.

8. When you are ready, take a grief class. It can help in practical ways. This is wise.

9. Tell your family where you are in your grief journey and that you do not need their counsel, just their love. This builds healthy boundaries.

10. Read the great saints of old who have suffered and lived to tell about it. This makes you a part of the community of faith and its continuing journey.

11. Be proactive with your friends. Don't wait for them to act.

As time passes, they will speak less and less of your loss, but this is natural and healthy. This is acceptance.

12. Proactively create your new life. It won't come automatically. Pray first, and then you can do anything that pleases God. This is good.

The longer I live, the more I learn; so this list will keep growing. Others who have trod the same path can add hundreds more of these guidelines, because God's care is wide, deep, and tailored to each person's individual grief.

CHAPTER 9

HOW DEATH CHANGED
THE WAY I LIVE

You who have shown me many troubles and
distresses
Will revive me again,
And will bring me up again from the depths of
the earth.
May You increase my greatness
And turn to comfort me.

—PSALM 71:20–21

These days when people ask me, "Pete, how are you doing?" I can honestly reply, "God has been good to me. He has carried me through the darkest part of grief. He has ended my search for *why?*, turned it into *what next?*, and given me a fresh picture of heaven that is the solid ground on which I am anticipating my future."

Please don't misunderstand me; I'm not saying my everyday life is wonderful now. After all, I'm a mere mortal with a broken heart. The lingering ache of grief is my new normal while I remain on earth. But here's the blessing of this reality: although I cannot maneuver around every heart-wrenching reminder of my past life with Harriet, the pain of her absence has given me X-ray vision of sorts. I see with different eyes—eyes that quickly recognize heartache in others. And I know that because of my experiences and the lessons I have learned about heaven, God can use me to help those struggling with loss, and they are everywhere.

My heartaches are being transformed from stumbling blocks to building blocks as I honestly share my story with those who have had to say "good-bye for now" to loved ones. This sharing has become part of my new normal, and I am gratified to know that God is able to use my pain to bless others struggling to understand their pain. Here are just a few of the notes I have received as a result of this new unsought ministry God has given me:

> I just wanted to drop you a note of thanks for being so open and honest with us last night; you certainly aren't obligated to do that. In telling us of what you have been through, you demonstrated how absolutely real Yahweh is for you and how firmly you are rooted in Christ.
>
> A new deacon

> My grandma passed away last year, and I have found so much comfort in the wisdom and stories you shared.
>
> A young student

> Hearing what you said about honesty in prayer has changed the way I communicate and view my personal relationship through prayer.
>
> A young student

I praise God for the testimony you have shared of how He has been so faithful to you in these promises. It has given me hope and encouraged me to trust Him more.

A YOUNG STUDENT

Thank you for being so genuine and transparent about your grief, suffering, and healing during these last few years. I can only hope to someday have the same kind of feelings and affections for my [future] wife that you still have for yours.

A YOUTH WORKER

Comments like these have made me realize that people identify far more readily with my suffering and weaknesses than they do with my strengths and successes. This has taught me that when I claim my grief, talk it out, or even write it out, then I can pray it out and share it. I'm not as afraid of grief now because I have experienced how the stumbling block of pain can become a building block of encouragement.

Faith Confirmed

My search for peace and relief has not been replaced or settled by my experiences; rather, my faith has been confirmed in the God who gave me these experiences. He is the same God who allowed His Son to suffer. Although the intensity lessens with time, heightened emotions are naturally a core aspect of such profound encounters. When Harriet's brother died, it bothered her that after a period of time people quit speaking of him. I felt the same way after Harriet's death. These days, she isn't discussed as much unless I bring her into a conversation. But I've learned that this is normal. One friend summed it up this way: "Life is for the living." I would amend that and say that life is *about* the living.

So I have learned to live in the present, not the past. I am comforted by knowing that the past is not lost in God's economy. Heaven will review and reward all that we have done on earth. Paul calls us to "be steadfast, immovable, always abounding in the work of the Lord, knowing that your toil is not in vain in the Lord" (1 Corinthians 15:58).

I have also learned to rest the past in God's hands. This was not an easy lesson, but it has proved a vital one for my spiritual, emotional, and mental health. With a kindred mind-set, David Ray wrote his poem "Thanks, Robert Frost," about America's poet laureate.

> Do you have hope for the future?
> Someone asked Robert Frost toward the end.
> "Yes, and even for the past," he replied,
> "That it will turn out to have been all right.
> For what it was, something we can accept,
> Mistakes made by the selves we had to be,
> Not able to be, perhaps, what we wished,
> Or what looking back half the time it seems
> We could so easily have been or ought . . .
> The future, yes, and even for the past,
> That it will become something we can bear."[1]

Nothing is wasted in the plan and providence of God. All our mistakes will become integral parts of the best patterns in the tapestry of our lives. All things will work together.

The wisdom I found in studying the Scriptures has helped me view life, death, and heaven in an altogether different way. And the lessons I learned both from my personal experiences and from reading many Christian authors reinforced these viewpoints.

Here is what I know for sure:

1. Death is not the end; it's a door to a bigger, better life.
2. Heaven is more magnificent than I ever imagined.
3. The reality of the better life that someday awaits me and all believers is what helps me grieve with hope and certainty.
4. Christ's resurrection is absolutely true, and now more valuable and vivid to me than ever.

Since Harriet's death, I have learned to accept mystery because I know there is meaning behind it. Just because I don't understand all that is happening right now doesn't mean it is purposeless or valueless. My God-given confidence in heaven has expanded my belief that my Harriet is not just okay; she is thriving! And someday I, too, will thrive in heaven.

Viewing heaven through the lens of biblical facts gave me permission to make logical deductions that have helped me to stand firm, even when my grief was at its heaviest. In addition, writers such as Francis Schaeffer and Randy Alcorn gave me the joy of using my imagination when thinking about heaven. Does not the apostle Paul also lead us in that direction?

Now to Him who is able to do far more abundantly beyond all that we ask or think [imagine], according to the power that works within us . . . (Ephesians 3:20)

> Things which eye has not seen and ear has not heard,
>
> And which have not entered the heart of man,
>
> All that God has prepared for those who love Him.
>
> (1 Corinthians 2:9)

Paul put it this way when he prayed for the Ephesian church: "I pray that the eyes of your heart may be enlightened, so that you will know what is the hope of His calling, what are the riches of the glory of His inheritance in the saints" (Ephesians 1:18).

Francis Schaeffer echoed Paul's affirmation of imagination as a means of perceiving truth when he wrote, "The Christian is the really free man—he is free to have imagination. This too is our heritage. The Christian is the one whose imagination should fly beyond the stars."[2]

Back Down to Earth

As much as I love thinking about heaven and dreaming of reuniting with Harriet, I exercise discipline to pull myself back down to earth. Why is this so important? Because these last few years have taught me that heaven is far more focused on earth than earth is focused on heaven. This truth has made the value of life in the here and now more vivid and meaningful.

What we do here on earth matters greatly to God. Genesis 1:28 teaches us that He created us to be His agents, His deputies on the earth: "Be fruitful and multiply, and fill the earth, and subdue it; and rule over the fish of the sea and over the birds of the sky and over every living thing that moves on the earth." God has honored us with the great responsibility of caring for His earth, shaping it, and using our gifts to advance His glory within it. Since mankind's fall in Eden, we have often performed this duty poorly, hampered by having to slog through the swamp of sin that is now part of our environment.

But the atoning sacrifice of Jesus has laid a solid foundation for us to build our work on. That work includes expanding His kingdom throughout the earth, demonstrating faith, ministering to the hurting, and using our gifts unselfishly to benefit others. The building we construct on Christ's foundation is critically important to God. Not only will it be carefully reviewed, but it will also be rewarded.

> For no man can lay a foundation other than the one which is laid, which is Jesus Christ. Now if any man builds on the foundation with gold, silver, precious stones, wood, hay, straw, each man's work will become evident; for the day will show it because it is to be revealed with fire, and the fire itself will test the quality of each man's work. If any man's work which he has built on it remains, *he will receive a reward.* (1 Corinthians 3:11–14)

Life on earth takes on greater importance when understood in the light of God's purposes and intentions. While we are here, we must embrace opportunities that glorify and please God. God is pleased when He sees us live by faith and take seriously our responsibility as His beloved agents in the earth.

The life of faith is integral to God's plan. James tells us that faith in God produces our desire to work in God's kingdom: "Faith by itself, if it is not accompanied by action, is dead" (2:17 NIV). I am learning to be more grateful for and more generous with what I have been given, as well as bolder in speaking about it.

Instruct those who are rich in this present world . . . to do good,
to be rich in good works, to be generous and ready to share,
storing up for themselves the treasure of a good foundation
for the future, so that they may take hold of that which is life
indeed. (1 Timothy 6:17–19)

Seeing life, death, and grief with new eyes has enabled me to
know God at a deeper level than I ever dreamed possible. When I
hurt the most, He revealed Himself the most. I discovered that the
purpose of the pain I felt was not to let me know how strong I was;
it was to enable me to discover how strong He is.

I also learned how critically important the church is. My con-
gregation held me close with their love. Besides visits, phone calls,
and letters throughout the last few years, their prayers sustained
me. It may sound odd to say that I felt those prayers, but I did. I felt
carried along on a wave of tender awareness of God. The constant
sense of His presence, compassion, and answer to almost every need
was beyond anything I had ever experienced. I truly believe that
all the compassion I received from heaven flowed because of those
prayers. In God's economy, there is no such thing as a small prayer.
Every prayer prayed is a grand testament to faith and love, and each
one is recorded in heaven. If we must give an account for every
"careless word" spoken (Matthew 12:36), then certainly we will be
blessed for every intentional word we speak in prayer for others.

One side benefit of my grief journey has been the outpour-
ing of appreciation for the love and work Harriet did on earth.
Granted, when a person dies, we tend to remember the best, and I
do not mean to mythologize my wife. She had her share of flaws.
She was often anxious, depressed, and weak. But this is where
grace reaches us at its best. God wants us to understand that His

strength is sufficient to carry us through in spite of our weaknesses: "My grace is sufficient for you, for power is perfected in weakness" (2 Corinthians 12:9). Harriet knew this. In fact, she once told a friend, "The holes we create in our children's lives by our mistakes create a need for God. If we were perfect, then they wouldn't know they needed God."

Holding on to this profound truth has helped me realize how influential believers can be in the lives of others. Everything we do on earth is important in God's eyes because we are made in His image. By our every act, we either tarnish that image or glorify it. Every part of this life that glorifies God points to something greater that exists above the life we experience here.

A thank-you note I found in Harriet's keepsakes is a legacy showing how her life mirrored God's image and declared His glory:

> Harriet, for the attention and support you gave me, I pray that it will be multiplied in your spiritual grandchildren and that you will be encouraged by knowing, on this side of heaven, that the efforts you make for the Lord's kingdom bear lasting fruit!

Another friend found the perfect words both to comfort me and to point to the legacy of love that links Harriet to her new life in heaven.

> Pete, Harriet is defined by her life, and not the darkness of her last moments of despair. The depth of the pain that we all feel today is proof that Harriet mattered in a profound way. Her legacy will never end, Pete. That is a small comfort, but dang, we all miss her so!

Randy Alcorn, a modern-day prophet, explained with great clarity the importance of cultivating our love for heaven:

Desire is a signpost pointing to Heaven. Every longing for better health is a longing for the perfect bodies we'll have on the New Earth. Every longing for romance is a longing for the ultimate romance with Christ. Every thirst for beauty is a thirst for Christ. Every taste of joy is but a foretaste of a greater and more vibrant joy than can be found on Earth now. . . .

Life on Earth matters, not because it's the only life we have, but precisely because it isn't. It's the beginning of a life that will continue without end on a renewed Earth.[3]

The death of my wife has completely changed my entire view of life. I can now honestly say and mean what Paul meant when he wrote, "For to me, to live is Christ and to die is gain" (Philippians 1:21). I'm still a sinner, yet my future death is as much a positive thing as my present life is. I am eager for heaven and will stand on God's truth until I get there. I am indeed living proof of those profound words spoken by the priest in the Superman movie *Man of Steel*: "Sometimes you have to take a leap of faith first. The trust part comes later."[4]

And trust has come. Praise God! My story would not be possible without His sacrifice for me or without the strength He supplies for my arduous journey.

> The Everlasting God, the LORD, the Creator of the ends
>   of the earth
> Does not become weary or tired.
> His understanding is inscrutable.

> He gives *strength* to the weary,
> And to him who lacks might He increases power. . . .
> Yet those who wait for the LORD
> Will gain *new strength*;
> They will mount up with wings like eagles,
> They will run and not get tired,
> They will walk and not become weary. (Isaiah 40:28–31)

At times, He has lifted me up and flown me with supernatural wings. At other times, He has strengthened me to run the race with power. Yet most of the time, He has simply walked with me and kept me from being weary—tired, yes, but not weary.

Thank You, Father! Thank You, Jesus! Thank You, Holy Spirit! Everything You promised, You have done—and so much more.

PART 3

WHAT EVERY
SEARCHING PERSON
NEEDS TO KNOW

CHAPTER 10

CLIMBING THE LADDER OF TRUTH

*It is not by thinking ourselves right that we cease to fear.
It is simply by loving and abandoning ourselves to Him
whom we love without returning to self. That is what
makes death sweet and precious. When we are dead to
ourselves the death of the body is only the consummation
of the work of grace.*

—FRANCIS FENELON, "ON DEATH"

God provided me with a way out of the abyss of grief by means of a ladder, much like the ladder from earth to heaven in Jacob's dream. It is what I call the Ladder of Truth, an instrument with seven critical rungs that lifted me out of my darkness and into the light from heaven. God provided the way, but it was up to me to make the climb.

I drew the courage to begin my climb from the peace that God had previously given me concerning Harriet's death. He takes responsibility for her death, and He has a purpose for it on which I can rest (Exodus 4:11; Job 42:11). God led my aching heart to the

Ladder of Truth. Buoyed by faith in that truth, I grasped the first rung and began my ascent.

Rung One: The Sovereignty of God

God initiated my climb with a question: *Pete, am I sovereign?* This is a profoundly important question, one that everyone must answer.

When I plunged into helplessness after the loss of Harriet, my belief in God's sovereignty was severely tested. *How can this be God's plan?* I wondered. *Harriet was my daily companion and my deepest confidant, and she has been ripped from my life. Is God in control?* I asked myself these questions again and again.

Even though my throbbing nerves screamed otherwise, I had to answer, *Yes, God is in control.* I did not base this confidence on my feelings; they were raw and wounded and ready to strike out at God for letting this thing happen to me. I based my belief in God's sovereignty on what I already knew about Him before Harriet died. That acknowledgment of God's absolute, unshakable sovereignty is the first rung of the Ladder of Truth.

The first rung of a ladder is the most important. Before you can begin climbing, you must believe that a ladder will bear your weight. You choose to commit to its foundational strength solely on that basis. Believing and acting on faith in my conviction that God is sovereign and fully in control gave me the courage, confidence, and core stability to begin climbing out of the abyss of grief.

Jesus reminds us in Matthew 19:26, "With God all things are possible." And Paul added, "God causes all things to work together for good to those who love God, to those who are called according to His purpose" (Romans 8:28). These biblical principles relating to

God's sovereignty are solid truths I knew I could trust, even when the weight of my grief was heavy. I firmly believed that God could and would work out Harriet's death and my resulting grief according to His purpose. How? I had no idea, but I knew He could.

I chose to put the full weight of my grief on that rung and stand on it with both feet. My confidence in God's sovereignty did not rest on my understanding of it; rather, my understanding—weak or absent as it was—rested on the fact that God *never* loses control.

RUNG TWO: THE GOODNESS OF GOD

To climb the Ladder of Truth, you have to keep moving up in faith. As I stood on that first rung, God asked me a second question: *Pete, am I good?*

Is God good? This question was far more difficult to answer—painful, in fact, given Harriet's suicide. I chewed on it far longer than I did the first question. If God is good, then why did this awful loss happen to me? Does He truly intend me good?

The question "Is God good?" begs another question: What does good really mean? Does it mean the same thing to me that it means to God? Apparently not, because my concept of good as it related to me meant that I should never have been deprived of Harriet. But if God is truly good and He allowed that loss to occur, then good must mean something to Him that was opaque to me.

Some theologians say that good can be best understood to mean "worthy of approval." Theologian Wayne Grudem, the author of *Systematic Theology*, asks a more appropriate question: "Approval by whom? . . . God's being and actions are perfectly worthy of his own approval. He is therefore the final standard of good."[1]

Jesus implied this profound truth in Mark 10:18 when He said,

119

"No one is good except God alone." If God is good—in fact, the only standard for good—then there must be some kind of good that will result from Harriet's death that is much greater than the good (as I perceived it) of having her remain as my companion. My realization of this truth changed my question from why to what. What sort of good could God be doing with my painful loss? Could He work Harriet's death for good—as He claims He is able to do?

So *why* was no longer the question. I knew I could not look to the future to answer, why did this awful thing happen? I could only look back in time to the what. I could look at examples of good things God had given to me in the past. And in my rearview mirror, His goodness was undeniable.

I had to answer without reservation, "Yes, God, You are good!" He brought me to Himself when I was a freshman at the University of Texas. He gave me a wife who wanted to be in the ministry with me. He gave us two beautiful daughters who love the Lord. He has given me incredible opportunities to teach all over the world. God's goodness to me is reflected in Psalm 31:19: "How great is Your goodness, which You have stored up for those who fear You, which You have wrought for those who take refuge in You!"

Yes, painful things had happened in my life that I could see no good in at the moment. But sometimes pain is necessary to bring about good. Removing a thorn from your foot can be extremely painful, but for the well-being of the foot, and to restore health, it must be removed.

With these two core questions answered, I was standing on the rung of God's sovereignty and gripping the rung of God's goodness—two rungs of solid, biblical truth. I was no longer looking down into the pit of my loss but gazing up to heaven with hope, much like Jacob had done in his dream in Genesis 28. Strength that I had lacked since Harriet's death surged through me. It was the same strength Abraham gained when he asked in Genesis 18:25, "Far be it from You! Shall not the Judge of all the earth deal justly?" The answer? "Absolutely!"

I knew God was saying to me, *You know I am sovereign, Pete. You know I am good. Now trust Me with what you do not understand. I am not finished yet!*

Perched on the Ladder of Truth between the dark abyss of grief and the light-filled reality of heaven, I was holding on to God with two confirmed insights: God is in absolute control, and God is good.

I recalled the line Harriet had marked in a passage by John Claypool: "The worst thing is not the last thing."[2] Even in the worst of evil, death does not have the final say. Death is not the end; it only appears that way to those of us still on earth. I love the way Dr. James Means explained this truth in his book *A Tearful Celebration*:

> He superintends all the events of my life so that His purposes might be achieved. This superintending grace of God includes even the events distasteful to me, but essential to His plan.
>
> Therefore, I hold God ultimately responsible for my grief because He is sovereign and has permitted cancer to prove fatal.[3]

Having Harriet as my companion and deepest confidant was exceptionally good, yet I did not realize just how blessed I was until I grasped the next rung of the Ladder of Truth.

Rung Three: Gratitude

The third rung of a ladder is the one that lifts you up to where you begin seeing things from a higher level. It's the rung that gives you an entirely different perspective. I was somewhat surprised to discover that on the Ladder of Truth, this perspective changer is the rung of gratitude.

John Claypool suffered the death of his ten-year-old daughter, Laura, and coping with this tragic loss became the subject of some of his books. I devoured these books on Harriet's bookshelf because I resonated with his pain. And in them I found the blessing that put me on the third rung of the ladder. Claypool helped me see the value of gratitude.

Writing after the death of his daughter, Claypool said this:

> I have two alternatives: I can dwell on the fact that she has been taken away, and dissolve in remorse that all of this is gone forever. Or, focusing on the wonder that she was ever given at all, I can resolve to be grateful that we shared life, even for an all-too-short ten years. There are only two choices here, but believe me, the best way out for me is the way of gratitude. The way of remorse does not alter the stark reality one whit and only makes matters worse. . . .
>
> Life is a gift—every particle of it, and . . . the way to handle a gift is to be grateful.[4]

The biblical word for gratitude is *thanksgiving*. Despite the dire circumstances of his life, the apostle Paul told believers, "In everything give thanks; for this is God's will for you in Christ Jesus" (1 Thessalonians 5:18). Gratitude for the hard things in life does not come as readily as gratitude for the pleasant things. But on a grief climb, gratitude must come early on; otherwise, the rungs above it are difficult to see.

I realized that to grasp the rung of gratitude fully, I had to ask myself this question: "When I think of Harriet, do I look down in self-pity or do I look up in gratitude to a sovereign God who intends me good?" Psalm 100:4–5 affirms that to embrace the vitality of life, even in the face of death, I must choose gratitude:

> Enter His gates with thanksgiving,
> And His courts with praise.
> Give thanks to Him, bless His name.
> For the LORD is good;
> His lovingkindness is everlasting
> And His faithfulness to all generations.

We must be committed to God's sovereignty and to His goodness (the first two rungs of the Ladder of Truth) in order to give thanks for the hard things in life. Isaiah 57:15 assures us that God will revive the heart that is humble toward Him:

> For thus says the high and exalted One
> Who lives forever, whose name is Holy,
> "I dwell on a high and holy place,
> And also *with the contrite and lowly of spirit*
> In order to revive the spirit of the lowly
> And to revive the heart of the contrite."

Gratitude is an odd way to climb out of darkness, isn't it? But I assure you, it works. The rung of gratitude is sturdy and uplifting. Early one morning a few weeks after Harriet's death, I sat by a fire and began to write in my journal why I was grateful for Harriet. Much to my surprise and joy, I noted fifty-nine gifts she gave me, such as lessons about life, a love of flowers, and appreciation of pain. I would not be the person I am today if Harriet had not given me those gifts. This list has grown over time, but when I initially compiled it, I was struck by a reality I had not seen before. The gifts Harriet had given me were God-ordained. Harriet was and always will be God's gift to me. As God brought Eve to Adam, God brought Harriet to me. Our romance began because God had her come to me. As I noted earlier, the first night we met, she went home and wrote in her diary, "I think I've met the man I want to marry." Sitting by that fire, I embraced the truth found in 1 Timothy 4:4: "For everything created by God is good, and nothing is to be rejected if it is received with gratitude." Second to my wonderful Savior, Harriet is God's greatest gift to me.

The rung of gratitude lifted me to a whole new vision for my future. Grief was not gone, but hope was getting stronger.

Rung Four: Life Is a Gift

"Life is a gift—every particle of it."[5] This profound observation is the next rung on the Ladder of Truth. The realization that life is a gift lifted me another step higher in my escape from the abyss of grief.

Here's the deal: no one deserves life. It is purely a gift from our loving God—and death shines a spotlight on just how precious life is. From the opening pages of Genesis, this truth is placed before us: "Then the LORD God formed man of dust from the ground, and breathed into his nostrils the breath of life; and man became a living being" (Genesis 2:7). This verse affirms that God gives us life, and Ecclesiastes 3:12–13 affirms that life is a gift: "I know that there is nothing better for them than to rejoice and to do good in one's lifetime; moreover, that every man who eats and drinks sees good in all his labor—it is the gift of God."

Gifts often come in unexpected packaging. In the three-month period from March through May 2013, I was asked to do six funerals. I had never officiated at that many funerals in a year, much less within a span of a few months. This stream of funerals began only three months after Harriet's death.

Leading these funerals did several things for me. It opened for me a new freedom to talk about life, heaven, and hope. I confess that speaking on these high subjects elevated my emotions to the point that in one funeral I waxed overly exuberant in extolling them. Perhaps I failed to attend properly to the grief that is part of such an occasion. But in subsequent funerals, I toned it down and found what I believe was a proper balance. After one of these funerals, a friend wrote the following note to me:

> Pete, the memorial service on Tuesday ranks among the finest
> I have ever had the privilege of hearing. Your heartfelt message
> was so rich with meaning and significance, as was your tribute.

I can truly say that the praise lavished in this note must go to God, not to me. I simply had the privilege of being His spokesperson by proclaiming what a glorious thing the gift of life truly is. And personally grasping this rung on the Ladder of Truth helped me immensely by lifting me one step higher on my ascent from the pit of grief.

Rung Five: Death Is a Gift

It may seem a paradox, but it's a biblical truth that just as life is a gift, so also is death. Grasping that strange fact puts us on the fifth rung of the Ladder of Truth. If you wonder how something as devastating as death could be a gift, read what the psalmist wrote in Psalm 116:15: "Precious in the sight of the LORD is the death of His godly ones."

Precious is an unusual word to connect with death. It means special and valuable. Even though death is called an enemy because it is the result of sin committed by Adam and Eve in the garden of Eden, the Scriptures give us several positive reasons for its existence. God ordained death to remain with us so that we would not live forever in our sin. Thus death became a gift, because unlimited life contaminated with sin would quickly become a cesspool of misery and hopelessness. This, as Scripture confirms, is the first reason for death:

> Then the LORD God said, "Behold, the man has become like one of Us, knowing good and evil; and now, he might stretch out his hand, and take also from the tree of life, and eat, and live forever"—therefore the LORD God sent him out from the garden of Eden, to cultivate the ground from which he was taken. So He drove the man out; and at the east of the garden of Eden He stationed the cherubim and the flaming sword which turned every direction to guard the way to the tree of life. (Genesis 3:22–24)

Death is the result of sin, but it also ends sin. Evidently God created Adam to live forever. But when Adam sinned, God removed from Eden the Tree of Life, which represented the sustaining fuel for Adam's eternal life. Now eternal life is found only in Christ's death and resurrection.

The second reason for death is that it reminds us that life is a test. At the heart of the test is whether we will use life to gain wisdom for God's purposes. We find this affirmed in Psalm 90:12: "So teach us to number our days, that we may present to You a heart of wisdom."

Third, death also reminds us that earthly life has limits: "As for the days of our life, they contain seventy years, or if due to strength, eighty years, yet their pride is but labor and sorrow; for soon it is gone and we fly away" (Psalm 90:10).

God sees death quite differently from the way we see it. Death is not a final destination; it is the door to our heavenly home. It is not a thief robbing us of love; it is a temporary separation. And when that separation comes, love doesn't cease to exist on either side of that thin veil between heaven and earth.

Finally, death has a goal. It brings us to our heavenly home and into the presence of our heavenly Father. Paul elaborated on this truth, using terms such as "house," "clothing," and "tent" as metaphors for our physical bodies:

> For indeed in this house we groan, longing to be clothed with our dwelling from heaven, inasmuch as we, having put it on, will not be found naked. For indeed while we are in this tent, we groan, being burdened, because we do not want to be unclothed but to be clothed, so that what is mortal will be swallowed up by life. Now He who prepared us for this very purpose is God, who gave to us the Spirit as a pledge.
>
> Therefore, [be] always of good courage . . . knowing that

while we are at home in the body we are absent from the Lord.
(2 Corinthians 5:2–6)

The gift of death, as Paul explained, is that when this body dies, we will be present with the Lord.

These reasons for death helped me see it as a gift—an unusual gift, to be sure, but one that creates a solid, biblical rung on the Ladder of Truth that gave me deep peace about Harriet's death. She is now free from sin, full of life, and at home with Christ. That is a beautiful picture I will hold in my heart until I once again see her face-to-face.

Rung Six: Grief Has a Purpose

Realizing that both life and death are gifts with purpose led me to the next rung of the Ladder of Truth: grief also has a purpose. Grief has been part of God's design since the fall of mankind in the garden of Eden. Grief exists only because God devised it as a necessary component of a fallen world. As the apostle John tells us, nothing exists apart from God: "All things came into being through Him, and apart from Him nothing came into being that has come into being" (John 1:3).

In 1 Peter 2:19 we are told, "For it is commendable if someone bears up under the pain of unjust suffering because they are conscious of God" (NIV). And Lamentations 3:31–38 speaks to God's sovereignty and His reluctant willingness to inflict pain, calamity, and grief when those modes of discipline will bring about the greatest good. Yet this passage also speaks to His mercy and the fact that in the wake of these afflictions He will pour out compassion and love:

For no one is cast off
> by the Lord forever.
Though he brings grief, he will show compassion,
> so great is his unfailing love.
For he does not willingly bring affliction
> or grief to anyone.

To crush underfoot
> all prisoners in the land,
to deny people their rights
> before the Most High,
to deprive them of justice—
> would not the Lord see such things?

Who can speak and have it happen
> if the Lord has not decreed it?
Is it not from the mouth of the Most High
> that both calamities and good things come? (NIV)

I had always thought of grief as an emotional result of loss. I had not seen it as something God brings.

Grief is the underside of love. It is the longing I have for Harriet—her smiling face, her warm presence, the sweet smell of her skin, and the sound of her laugh. It brings an emptiness I have to face. In John 12:24 Jesus explained death with an allegory: "Unless a grain of wheat falls into the earth and dies, it remains alone."

All earthly life and love must die—not because they aren't good, but because they aren't complete. The husk of the old sin nature we inherited from Adam must be shed. That is the death of the "earth suit," so to speak, and this shedding has to happen before a believer can be given a new resurrected body, which will enable him to live and love perfectly.

Life and love as currently perceived are mere shadows of the real things to come in heaven. They will not be different things, but better and bigger realities of the old things! Harriet did not cease to be Harriet when she died; she became the *real* Harriet, the perfect Harriet, the complete Harriet. She still has the same smile, laugh, and beauty she had on earth, but she is totally free of all hindrances of the old life.

This same transformation will happen to every person who dies embracing the redemption provided by Jesus Christ. As much as I grieve Harriet's absence on earth, the sixth rung of the Ladder of Truth taught me to celebrate her newfound perfection in heaven, especially knowing that one day I will join her in that perfection.

Rung Seven: Anticipation

As I climbed the ladder, truth was peeling off layers of my grief rung by rung. Please note that the ascent from grief is never fully complete on this side of heaven. Grief fulfills its purpose in shielding us from the sting of death. It is an ever-present environment, much like being in a womb. You feel enclosed, maybe even trapped. When the worst of grief ends, it doesn't mean happiness immediately begins, because the empty space left by the life that has gone remains.

But this emptiness also has a positive function. It is a form of waiting, a form of anticipation, which is the seventh rung of the Ladder of Truth. Waiting and anticipating are part of the God-ordained cycle of planting, watering, weeding, and fertilizing. We commit ourselves to these facets of cultivation, and then we wait until the season of fruit returns so we can reap the harvest. God has created us to bear fruit, and often the fruit of sorrow becomes our best offering to Him.

This rung of anticipation is mounted on the steadfast love of the Lord, which never ceases because His mercies are new every morning (Lamentations 3:23). The emptiness created in my life by Harriet's death is achingly real, but the waiting period before I reunite with her in heaven is not wasted time. As I wait and anticipate, God is at work in me.

In Psalm 3:5, David wrote, "I lay down and slept; I awoke, for the LORD sustains me." He added in Psalm 121:3, "He who keeps you will not slumber." Then in Psalm 5:3, David spoke of anticipation: "In the morning, O LORD, You will hear my voice; in the morning I will order my prayer to You and eagerly watch." This same hope David had, firmly rooted in the steadfast love of God, is the anticipation that lifted me from the darkness of grief into heaven's sunlight.

I learned so much while climbing the Ladder of Truth. When I stood upright on the top rung, I saw life and death from a totally different perspective. And I saw heaven differently too. I realized that my previous perspective of heaven had been pitifully small, one-dimensional, and shallow. I had not seen heaven as the glorious, incredible, solid ground that it truly is.

Climbing out of the pit did not mean my journey had ended. By God's love and mercy, each rung is merely a steppingstone to new understanding of greater realities. This continual unfolding reminded me of a Russian doll. It looks complete on the surface, but it opens up to reveal another doll inside. You repeat the process several times, and to your surprise, each time yet another doll emerges.

As I dismounted the ladder, before me opened a new vista revealing ten realities about heaven that I was yet to discover. I set out to explore those realities, and each new discovery brought me joy and excitement I had not felt since before Harriet's death. I will reveal what I discovered in the next two chapters.

CHAPTER 11

AMAZING HEAVEN—
ITS SETTING

*Little faith will bring the soul to heaven, but much faith
will bring heaven to the soul.*
—CHARLES SPURGEON, QUOTED IN ELISABETH
ELLIOT, *SHADOW OF THE ALMIGHTY*

After climbing the Ladder of Truth, I was finally at peace about
Harriet's death, and I became intensely interested in her new
life. I cannot imagine a more enthusiastic citizen of heaven than
Harriet. While she was on earth, her enthusiasm for the smallest of
things made a huge difference in the lives of others. One friend said
of her, "Harriet will certainly make heaven a more lively place!"
Even before Harriet left the earth, she was primed to be a citizen of
heaven. She exuded the aroma that makes heaven heavenly.

Thinking about Harriet living in heaven sparked my curiosity and motivated me to discover all I could about our eternal
home and the life we will live there. I had read Randy Alcorn's
book *Heaven* several years before Harriet's death.[1] It is the most
thorough, biblically based work ever written on the subject, and it
opened my eyes to many new insights about the nature of heaven.

I went to the library at my seminary, found fifty books on the subject of heaven and the afterlife, and read them all. Several of these books rose to the top as the best both biblically and scholarly, including but not limited to *Probing Heaven* by John Gilmore, *Exploring Heaven* by Arthur O. Roberts, and *Everything You Ever Wanted to Know About Heaven* by Peter Kreeft.[2]

I did not want the wisdom of men, however, to mislead me in my quest for truth about heaven. I was determined that everything I committed to my mind would be based on God's Word. I was acutely aware that in my distraught state, I could easily allow my imagination to run ahead of revealed truth, causing me to construct fanciful castles in the air and call them heaven.

So, as I delved into the wisdom of these books, I prayerfully took care to ground my research in the Scriptures. As Jesus told us, "If you continue in My word, then you are truly disciples of Mine; and you will know the truth, and the truth will make you free" (John 8:31–32).

The purpose of my quest was to discover what truths we can discern about life in heaven that will encourage us on earth, especially when we are grieving the death of a loved one. The truths in this chapter and the next have given me peace about Harriet's death, joy for the life she now lives, and great expectations for the eternal life that awaits me. I invite you to walk with me through these healing and encouraging truths I learned about heaven. The first four truths, discussed in this chapter, help us gain the big picture.

Heaven Is a Literal Place

I am continually surprised at how many Christians think heaven is some kind of vague, ethereal environment where we will exist in some mode that is not physical. In their minds, there is nothing solid about heaven. They believe that neither heaven nor our bodies will be physical realities. Popular imagery has led many to perceive heaven as consisting of little more than clouds and a pearly gate.

Jesus firmly discredited this misconception of heaven when he told the repentant thief on the cross, "Today you shall be with Me in Paradise" (Luke 23:43). He was referring to a place, not a theological or philosophical concept. Throughout Scripture the word "Paradise" always means an actual place.

When Jesus told His disciples, "I go and prepare a place for you" (John 14:3), He used the Greek word *topon*, which means "place." The word *topography* is derived from *topos*. Heaven has topography. It is an actual landscape that can be mapped and traveled. Jesus confirmed the reality of heaven by adding, "that where I am, there you may be also." If heaven were not an actual place, Jesus would either be misleading His disciples or careless in His choice of words, both of which are impossible for the perfect Son of God to do.

In his book *Probing Heaven*, John Gilmore affirmed the literal reality and solidity of heaven:

> Three serious arguments . . . commend and make credible heaven as a place. First, God is said to have created heaven as well as earth. How could God have created something that can't be located? The second reason . . . : Christ ascended with a resurrection body. How can a body that was tangible, that took up space, not exist in a heavenly place? Third, there are specific texts, both in the Old Testament and in the New Testament, which speak of heaven as a place.[3]

Isaiah 57:15 confirms heaven as an actual place—in fact, it is the dwelling place for God, who said to Isaiah, "I dwell on a high and holy place."

Ezekiel 28:13–16 shows us that heaven existed in eternity past when the angels were created. We also know that heaven currently exists, as implied by Jesus to the thief on the cross. And according to Revelation 2:7, it also exists in the future: "To him who overcomes, I will grant to eat of the tree of life which is in the Paradise of God."

The Bible describes heaven as three distinct things: a kingdom (Matthew 4:17), a country (Hebrews 11:13–16), and a city (Hebrews 11:10; 12:22–24; 13:14). The apostle John affirmed the reality of heaven as a kingdom by telling us that it contains a throne with a king sitting on it (Revelation 5:1). As a country, it is filled with rivers and trees (Revelation 22:1–3), and one can easily envision surrounding hills and meadows. In its city, there are streets (Revelation 22:2), banquet rooms, and sources of food (Isaiah 25:6; Matthew 8:11; Revelation 19:9). Each of these descriptions shouts the fact that heaven is a rock-solid, tangible reality. This truth could hardly be made more explicit.

The reality of heaven makes even more sense when we read that the New Jerusalem will one day come down out of heaven to make its home on earth.

> And I saw the holy city, new Jerusalem, coming down out of heaven from God, made ready as a bride adorned for her husband. And I heard a loud voice from the throne, saying, "Behold, the tabernacle of God is among men, and He will dwell among them, and they shall be His people, and God Himself will be among them." . . .

> And he carried me away in the Spirit to a great and high
> mountain, and showed me the holy city, Jerusalem, *coming
> down out of heaven from God*. (Revelation 21:2–3, 10)

Consider the illogic of a symbolic or metaphoric city descending to a real and solid earth. When two conflicting concepts meet, one or the other must be the product of erroneous thinking. Both heaven and earth must be real, or both must be fantasy, or one could not merge into the other. We know by our own existence that earth is real, and by the rules of logic, that means that heaven must also be real. Otherwise, what exists in one place could not find a home in the other.

Many Christians think the descriptions in the book of Revelation are symbolic and too enigmatic to be understood. Some pastors and teachers treat the book as little more than stylized apocryphal literature filled with poetic metaphors. To dismiss the book in such a cavalier way is shortsighted and misleading, because we find the concepts presented in Revelation integrated throughout Scripture. The book of Revelation does contain metaphors, yet not everything described must be a metaphor. Metaphors are usually clearly recognized by how they're presented.

Even if one takes the position that the images in Revelation are metaphors, that does not dismiss their reality. A metaphor has to mean something. It is not a fictional substitute for reality; it displays reality in colorful dress to make it more vivid. In Scripture, however, heaven is almost always spoken of in plain, direct language that leaves no rationale for interpreting it metaphorically. The same goes for descriptions of the elements that characterize heaven—the kingdom, the city, the country, the throne, and the king. All of these are concrete realities existing in a real place. If for no other reason, we know it is real because Jesus said it is real.

Heaven and Earth Are Near to Each Other

This truth about heaven is one of my favorites: heaven is near to earth. As I mentioned, shortly after Harriet's death I visited our cabin in the woods. While sitting at the dining table, I noticed a wooden plaque hanging on the wall. Harriet must have purchased it, but she had never mentioned it and I had never noticed it until then. These words are etched into the wood of the plaque: "The Parting Wall."

On the plaque is a man on one side of a thin wall and his wife on the other side. The two are close to each other but still separated. I began to wonder, *Is Harriet as close to me as the mere width of a thin wall? Are heaven and earth actually touching, separated by only a thin barrier? If so, are there openings in that wall through which connections might be made?*

I mentioned the proximity of heaven to earth in chapter 1, but now I want to reveal to you solid biblical reasons that I know their nearness to be a reality. I went to the Bible for answers, and what I found left no room for doubt: heaven and earth are touching. Consider the following scriptures, and notice the focus on "near":

You are *near*, O Lord, and all Your commandments are truth. (Psalm 119:151)

Seek the Lord while He may be found; call upon Him while He is *near*. (Isaiah 55:6)

The LORD looks from heaven;
He sees all the sons of men;
From his dwelling place he looks out
On all the inhabitants of the earth,
He who fashions the hearts of them all,
He who understands all their works. (Psalm 33:13–15)

In the book *We Shall See God*, edited by Randy Alcorn, the famous nineteenth-century evangelist Charles Spurgeon supports the concept of heaven's nearness to earth.

Between Earth and Heaven there is but a thin partition. The home country is much nearer than we think. Heaven is by no means the far country, for it is the Father's house.

Heaven is, at any rate, so near that in a moment we can speak with Him . . .

Oh, brothers and sisters, we are within hearing of the shining ones.[4]

In a singular reversal of the citizens of heaven observing those of us on earth, the account of the stoning of Stephen shows us a man on earth seeing inhabitants of heaven. Though this seems to be a one-of-a-kind incident, it, too, gives us biblical confirmation of heaven's nearness.

But being full of the Holy Spirit, he *gazed intently into heaven* and saw the glory of God, and Jesus standing at the right hand of God; and he said, "Behold, I see the heavens opened up and the Son of Man standing at the right hand of God." (Acts 7:55–56)

Scripture also confirms the nearness of heaven and earth by telling us that those in heaven can see and hear some of what happens here, including moments of repentance: "I tell you, there is joy in the presence of the angels of God over one sinner who repents" (Luke 15:10). This verse is commonly interpreted to mean that angels rejoice when someone accepts the forgiveness of Christ. And they likely do so. However, the phrasing "there is joy in the presence of the angels" actually communicates the idea that others besides the angels are experiencing joy. What group is most likely to celebrate repentance with unfettered joy? Those in heaven who have experienced repentance and its result: eternal life in a breathtakingly beautiful heaven. Knowing my enthusiastic Harriet, when she sees these glimpses of repentance of earth, her joy cup runs over in heaven.

In John 8:56, Jesus told the Jewish leaders who were harassing Him, "Your father Abraham rejoiced to see My day, and he saw it and was glad." Jesus was confirming that Abraham, who had died centuries before Christ was born on earth, was able to see and rejoice in the presence of Jesus here. Obviously, Abraham witnessed this event from his viewpoint in heaven.

Hebrews 12:1 also speaks to the reality of those in heaven viewing events on earth:

> Therefore, since we have so great a cloud of witnesses *surrounding us*, let us also lay aside every encumbrance and the sin which so easily entangles us, and let us run with endurance the race that is set before us.

The word "surrounding" in this verse is derived from the word for *amphitheater*, which supports the athletic imagery used here.

The idea is that those who have already run their race are now watching us as we run ours. B. F. Westcott, in his commentary on the book of Hebrews, added, "Those champions of old time occupy the place of spectators, but they are more than spectators. . . . The word *perikeimenon* [surrounding] gives the thought of the great company to whom the Christian athlete is made a spectacle."[5]

The testimony of both Scripture and theologians makes it clear that those in heaven are watching earth closely. In fact, earth seems to be a central focus of the heavenly inhabitants. This should not surprise us, for God is at work carrying out His plan for the redemption of the earth, which includes uniting heaven and earth into a single entity. This plan began in Genesis 1:26:

> Then God said, "Let Us make man in Our image, according to Our likeness; and let them *rule* over the fish of the sea and over the birds of the sky and over the cattle and over all the earth, and over every creeping thing that creeps on the earth."

The fulfillment of the plan, as evidenced by the word "rule" in Genesis, is seen in the word "reign" in Revelation 20:6:

> Blessed and holy is the one who has a part in the first resurrection; over these the second death has no power, but they will be priests of God and of Christ and will *reign* with Him for a thousand years.

In 2 Timothy 2:12, the apostle Paul added, "If we endure, we will also reign with Him." We can see that mankind reigning over the earth was God's plan from the beginning, and it remains His plan in the future. If care of the earth is infused into mankind's creation and continues in eternity, then it makes little sense to think it is not the duty of humans now—both those of us on the earth as well as those in heaven. Therefore, it makes perfect sense that as part of God's kingdom and His ambassadors, the citizens of heaven are intensely interested in our work on earth. Indeed, it appears that even in heaven they continue to perform the function God charged humans with originally in Eden: the citizens of heaven are still acting as caretakers of the earth with their visitations and their prayers.

In light of these truths, it is both biblical and logical to assume that the saints in heaven, as a part of the body of Christ, are interested in us and actively participate in our well-being. They have not forgotten us, and they pray about things on earth.

I have studied Scripture intensely to understand the interaction of the saints in heaven (sometimes called the *church victorious*) and the saints on earth (sometimes called the *church militant*). It is apparent that those in heaven pray for us because their lives and memories continue in a perfected state, which means they are aware of us. They are aware of our prayers:

> When He had taken the book, the four living creatures and the twenty-four elders fell down before the Lamb, each one holding a harp and golden bowls full of incense, which are the *prayers of the saints*. (Revelation 5:8)

Notice the emphasis on quantity: "bowls full."

> Another angel came and stood at the altar, holding a golden censer; and much incense was given to him, so that he might add

it to the *prayers of all the saints* on the golden altar which was before the throne. (Revelation 8:3)

Notice the emphasis that "all the saints" were praying.

And they cried out with a loud voice, saying, "How long, O Lord, holy and true, will You refrain from judging and avenging our blood on those who dwell on the earth?" (Revelation 6:10)

They are also aware of the sufferings they experienced on earth.

It appears that in heaven our loved ones pray even more for us than they did while on earth. Given their perfected state, this is not surprising. Harriet prayed for me every day of our life together on earth. Why would she do any less in heaven? J. Sidlow Baxter affirmed this enhanced intensity of prayer in his book *The Other Side of Death*:

All his people who have joined him then are now exercising *their* now-elevated priesthood as his privileged cointercessors, interceding for us who are still on earth. . . . Your treasured one yonder is thinking of you, loving you, *praying* for you; praying for you continually with such enlightened understanding that every such intercession is answered with a divine "Yes," and registers itself in sustenance and blessing which come to you daily.[6]

In *Surprised by Hope*, N. T. Wright explained this interaction:

Since both the departed saints and we ourselves are in Christ, we share them then in the "communion of saints." They are still our brothers and sisters in Christ. When we celebrate the Eucharist they are there with us, along with the angels and archangels. Why then should we not pray for and with them?[7]

Wright added for clarity that nowhere in Scripture are we encouraged to pray to the saints to intercede for us. The Reformers were adamant about this because of the fallacy of purgatory, which enjoined earthly saints to pray for their loved ones to be released from this supposed intermediate state. But he added:

Once we rule out purgatory, I see no reason why we should not pray for and with the dead and every reason why we should . . . that they will be refreshed and filled with God's joy and peace. Love passes into prayer; we still love them; why not hold them, in that love, before God?[8]

This truth about the nearness of heaven to earth has solidified my belief that not only are the two entities near but they are intricately connected. And as God allows, our loved ones in heaven are aware of our actions on earth. They pray for us and cheer us on in every way God in His wisdom allows. Harriet was my ministry partner on earth, and I believe she continues to cheer me on in heaven. How comforting!

HEAVEN IS BEAUTIFUL

Jesus confirmed the beauty of heaven by describing it as Paradise. *Paradise* is an ancient word meaning a "walled garden," which confirms the biblical connection between the garden of Eden and

Paradise, a synonym for heaven. This connection becomes clear when we compare the two following passages, one at the beginning of the Bible and the other at the end:

> The LORD God planted a garden toward the east, in Eden; and there He placed the man whom He had formed. Out of the ground the LORD God caused to grow every tree that is pleasing to the sight and good for food; the tree of life also in the midst of the garden, and the tree of the knowledge of good and evil. (Genesis 2:8–9)

> "He who has an ear, let him hear what the Spirit says to the churches. To him who overcomes, I will grant to eat of the tree of life which is in the Paradise of God." (Revelation 2:7)

The presence of the Tree of Life in both Genesis and Revelation confirms the intimate connection between Eden and Paradise. Both are gardens, places of extreme beauty and immense delight. Eden is described as a place where the trees were pleasing to the sight and good for food; a place of rivers; a place with gold and beautiful stones; and a place of birds and animals (Genesis 2). A verse in Ezekiel reveals to us that Eden existed even before God created the earth. When God created Lucifer, who was one of the highest orders of angels, this once-beautiful creature was in this heavenly Eden. "You were in Eden, the garden of God" (Ezekiel 28:13).

This order of creation—the garden of Eden that first existed in heaven and then was later replicated on earth—is confirmed in Job 38:7 when God tells Job that as He finished creation, "The morning stars sang together and all the sons of God shouted for joy." The "stars" in this verse refer to angels, because actual stars do not sing. The fact that *all* the angels are rejoicing at creation reveals that Lucifer had not yet fallen.

All of this tells me that Eden and Paradise are similar, if not the same, and that Eden was a beautiful place God made for His creatures and Himself to enjoy together. I have always loved Genesis 3:8 because of what it represents: "They heard the sound of the LORD God walking in the garden in the cool of the day." What a wonderful picture of God enjoying the beauty and richness of His creation!

In his book *The Divine and the Human*, Russian religious philosopher Nicolas Berdyaev tells us that Eden, or Paradise, is the root source of the beauty that remains in our fallen world: "All beauty in the world is either a memory of Paradise or a prophecy of the transfigured world."[9]

Jonathan Edwards described the unending beauty of our heavenly home this way in his book *Heaven: A World of Love*: "How soon do earthly lovers come to an end of their discoveries of each other's beauty; how soon do they see all there is to be seen! But in Heaven there is with new beauties always being discovered."[10]

Since heaven is a perfect place created by a perfect God, it's certain that when we enter heaven we will be perfected as well. All the flaws we inherited from Adam will be corrected, and we will become what we were intended to be from the beginning. C. S. Lewis once commented that if a citizen of heaven were to return to earth to visit us, we would be tempted to fall low and worship that individual. Harriet has always been beautiful to me. I can't imagine how much more beautiful she has become as a resident of a breathtaking heaven.

Heaven Is a Mystery

Ah, mystery! It keeps us enthralled, doesn't it? Paul wrote often of the mystery of God and quoted Isaiah to remind us that we have not yet seen or heard all that God has yet to reveal to us: "Things which eye has not seen and ear has not heard, and which have not entered the heart of man, all that God has prepared for those who love Him" (1 Corinthians 2:9).

The reason much of heaven is shrouded in mystery is simple. It is to whet our appetites. If we presently earthbound creatures could fully comprehend the reality of heaven, then we would do everything in our power to get there as quickly as possible. Complete knowledge of such glory would draw our focus from the importance of our duties on earth. While heaven is our goal, God has placed us on earth to achieve His purpose. This means our earthly journey is just as important as our final destination—not as glorious, but nevertheless as important. We are given hints of heavenly glory to draw us forward, but its mystery is retained to prevent distraction from our present purpose.

We are placed on earth to accomplish things that bring God glory, not only on earth but also in heaven. Paul reminds us in Ephesians 2:7 that God will display us as His trophies of grace to all of the heavenly realm "so that in the ages to come He might show the surpassing riches of His grace in kindness toward us in Christ Jesus." This verse tells us that we have opportunities here on earth to bring God glory in heaven. It is yet another indication that the veil between heaven and earth is thin and permeable.

Paul, with his intimate connection and interchanges with God, no doubt understood much more of heaven's mystery than we do. He even debated whether it would be better to depart and be with Christ or continue having fruitful labor here (Philippians 1:21–24). He said to be with Christ was by far better, but to continue to serve on earth was necessary.

As the Bible tells us, heaven is full of glorious mysteries presently hidden from us. However, these mysteries will not remain hidden forever. They are glories that will someday be revealed to us in person, and we will experience them as realities forever.

I am deeply gratified to know that Harriet lives in such an eternal and beautiful place, along with every believer who has left this earth. The mystery of her new life and role in heaven excites me to no end because the work of God is eternal and therefore inexhaustible. Just as I will remain in awe of the unfolding beauty of God for all eternity, Scripture makes it clear that I will also enjoy the beautiful, eternal, unfolding mysteries of Harriet and all the other saints in heaven.

CHAPTER 12

AMAZING HEAVEN—
ITS PEOPLE

*We will do many of the same things in Heaven that we did
here on earth—just perfectly.*

—STEVEN J. LAWSON, *HEAVEN HELP US!*

I n the previous chapter, I presented the first four of the ten truths
about heaven I discovered in my studies. Those truths had to do
with heaven as a place and its interconnections with earth. The
remaining six truths in this chapter reveal the characteristics and
activities of heaven's inhabitants.

THE PURITY OF HEAVEN'S CITIZENS

Although our lives continue after we leave earth, there is one vast
difference. On earth our lives are contaminated by the sin nature we
inherited from Adam. In heaven that nature will be left behind and
we will be perfectly pure. We "shed our old sin skin," so to speak. In
Romans 7:15, Paul acknowledged the burden of the sin nature: "For
what I am doing, I do not understand; for I am not practicing what
I would like to do, but I am doing the very thing I hate."

In heaven the conflict that caused Paul such angst is gone, because perfection—gained through the sacrifice of God's sinless Son—has displaced it. The writer of Hebrews celebrated this perfection:

> But you have come to Mount Zion and to the city of the living God, the heavenly Jerusalem, and to myriads of angels, to the general assembly and church of the firstborn who are enrolled in heaven, and to God, the Judge of all, and to *the spirits of the righteous made perfect*, and to Jesus, the mediator of a new covenant, and to the sprinkled blood, which speaks better than the blood of Abel. (12:22–24)

Charles Spurgeon said this about heaven:

> When Christ's followers rise, they shall leave the old Adam behind them. Blessed day! One of the happiest aspects of Heaven will be freedom from the tendency to sin, a total death to that old nature which has been our plague and woe.[1]

The apostle John confirmed this attained perfection:

> Beloved, now we are children of God, and it has not appeared as yet what we will be. We know that when He appears, we will be like Him, because we will see Him just as He is. And everyone who has this hope fixed on Him *purifies himself, just as He is pure.* (1 John 3:2–3)

To "be like Him" means we will be pure as Christ is pure. In his book *Exploring Heaven*, Arthur O. Roberts used the lens of logic and reason to reach this conclusion about life in heaven: "Without sin to corrupt and destroy, we can handle enhanced sensory perceptions, we can make judgments from a cleansed mind, and we can express our emotions from clarified intuitions."[2]

This must be in part what Paul meant when he told the Ephesian church that God chose us so that we "would be holy and blameless before Him" (Ephesians 1:4), "having no spot or wrinkle" (Ephesians 5:27). I have tried to think of Harriet without a sin nature, without a spot or wrinkle, her spirit made perfect. What is that like? At the least, it means she has no fear; she is confident but humble; she is eager to serve and worship. She is full of joy, never worries, is never discouraged, is always free to share her heart, and on and on. I can hardly wait to see her and experience the freedom and joy she now has! She has become pure.

THE ACTIVITY OF HEAVEN

In Jesus' parable of the talents, the master compliments the servant for being faithful in a few things and then tells him that because of his faithfulness, he will be put in charge of many things (Matthew 25:14–30). The parable is clearly speaking of heaven. Since parables illustrate truth, this one tells us that we will be given tasks to perform in heaven. It will be a place of highly meaningful activity.

At the close of the book of Revelation, John wrote, "There will no longer be any curse; and the throne of God and of the Lamb will be in it, and His bond-servants will serve Him" (Revelation 22:3). "Serve" is an action word. Since Revelation 21 tells us that heaven and earth will be reunited, this means there will be amazing opportunities for believers to embrace in this perfect new environment. Certainly we will worship God and Jesus face-to-face, but that is not all we will do. God created humans to be active, and as in the parable of the talents, He will give us meaningful assignments in heaven. Everything we accomplish there will be to Him an act of praise and worship.

For most of us, the common conception of heaven as a place of idleness is hardly appealing. When we remain idle, we get bored. We need not worry about boredom in heaven. Heaven is not an elaborate retirement center. It's a place where we will reflect and supplement God's creativity.

In his book *Heaven Help Us!* Steven J. Lawson wrote, "Actually we will do many of the same things in Heaven that we did here on earth—just perfectly."[3] I am confident that Harriet is extremely active in heaven and most likely enthralled by immersion into her favorite vocation—creating beauty with flowers. Harriet often said, "When you look into the face of a flower, you see the love of our Creator, God." She saw flowers as a way to exalt God. Why would she not continue to use flowers to exalt God in heaven?

In his book *Biblical Teaching on the Doctrines of Heaven and Hell*, pastor Edward Donnelly supported the concept of meaningful activity in heaven. He wrote, "Throughout eternity we will live full, truly human lives, exploring and managing God's creation to his glory. Fascinating vistas will unfold before us as we learn to serve God in a renewed universe."[4]

When Isaiah spoke of the glorious future awaiting in the new heaven and new earth, he said the inhabitants will build houses and plant vineyards, and that none of their labor will be in vain. This implies wonderful, joyful activity yet to come that cannot be undone by the destructive effects of the Fall.

They will build houses and inhabit them;

They will also plant vineyards and eat their fruit.

They will not build and another inhabit,

They will not plant and another eat;

For as the lifetime of a tree, so will be the days of My people,

And My chosen ones will wear out the work of their hands.

    (Isaiah 65:21–22)

Dallas Willard put it so well: "Your eternal destiny is not cosmic retirement; it is to be part of a tremendously creative project, under unimaginably splendid leadership, on an inconceivable scale, with ever-increasing cycles of fruitfulness and enjoyment—that is the prophetic vision which 'eye has not seen nor the ear has heard.'"[5]

Biblical fact, as well as reason and logic, confirm that life in heaven is full of activity that all its inhabitants embrace with gusto and without fatigue. What a wonderful world to look forward to!

THE WISDOM AND KNOWLEDGE OF HEAVEN'S CITIZENS

Although we do not become omniscient when we enter heaven, our knowledge and wisdom will blossom exponentially. One source of our wisdom will be God's law. Although it was initially given to us on earth, Psalm 119 tells us that God's law is eternal in nature—still valid in heaven:

So I will keep Your law continually,

Forever and ever . . .

Forever, O LORD,
Your word is settled in heaven. (vv. 44, 89)

From these verses we can reason that in heaven we will continue to study, learn, and meditate on God's Word. We will increase in our knowledge forever because we serve an infinite God. Can you imagine being able to sit down with Old Testament prophets and asking them to explain what they wrote? God's wisdom will never be exhausted. As New Testament scholar William Hendricksen expressed it:

> According to Scripture, when the soul enters heaven it continues to live. . . . It lives more abundantly than ever before. Now *to live* means to think, to have fellowship, to see and hear, to rejoice, etc. . . . Is it at all probable that we shall think and not advance in *knowledge*? . . . just as the "perfect" Christ-child was the one who "*advanced* in wisdom and stature, and in favor with God and men."[6]

Here's another exciting truth about wisdom in heaven: we will fully understand the purpose and context of our earthly lives. "Each man's work will become evident; for the day will show it because it is to be revealed with fire, and the fire itself will test the quality of each man's work" (1 Corinthians 3:13).

I am confident that Harriet now understands why God allowed depression to enter her life. She sees the entire tapestry, not just the portion of fabric that was her earthly life. I also believe that daily she is gaining knowledge of other aspects of God's divine plan, and this newly gained knowledge is far more abundant than that represented by the books in her bookshelves on earth. Even more important, she has begun to explore God in an intensely personal way and to enjoy Him forever. This gives me great peace.

All our thoughts will one day have the clarity of heaven and the perspective of eternity. Paul's words in 1 Corinthians 13:12 speak volumes about how greatly our knowledge and wisdom will expand in heaven: "For now we see in a mirror dimly, but then face to face; now I know in part, but then I will know fully just as I also have been fully known."

THE CONTINUITY OF HEAVENLY LIVES

Probably no truth about heaven has helped me through my personal grief more than the truth of continuity. The continuity of life as it moves from earth to heaven is a clear fact of Scripture. Jesus told His disciples that He looked forward to drinking the fruit of the vine with them in His Father's kingdom (Matthew 26:29). It's as if He were saying, "I've enjoyed this, but I have to leave for a while. When you meet Me there, let's do this again." We know that the disciples' earthly friendship with God's Son continues in heaven to this day because Jesus specifically promised it. The Jesus whom the disciples met after His death and resurrection is the same person they walked with on earth for three years. He knew them by face and called them by name. How can we doubt that Jesus and His disciples are continuing to enjoy the relationship He initiated on earth even as you read this page?

This promise of relationship continuity assures me that in heaven I will know Harriet by face and name. Our continuity as the same persons will enable us to experience the same love we had on earth, only now even better. The question naturally arises: Will a person still be married in heaven? This demands a more thorough study of Matthew 22:23–30, where Jesus is asked that very question. Briefly, the answer is twofold. The old, earthly form of marriage as a contract will no longer exist (Romans 7:1–2). And both the tensions created from the Fall and the sin natures that exist between a man and a woman (outlined in Genesis 3:7, 16; 1 Peter 3:1, 7) must die. Yet the marriage relationship will continue and thrive. No matter how good our love for each other was on earth, it will not begin to compare to the perfect love that will cast out all fear in heaven. This is what God will add to our relationship in heaven.

Genesis 25:8 speaks of this eternal link of loved ones between heaven and earth: "Abraham breathed his last and died in a ripe old age, an old man and satisfied with life; and he was gathered to his people." Some might think this verse refers to Abraham's being buried in the same place as his relatives, but we know it means far more because Jesus made it clear in Matthew 8:11 that we will sit at the table with Abraham and his loved ones in heaven: "I say to you that many will come from east and west, and recline at the table with Abraham, Isaac and Jacob in the kingdom of heaven."

Jesus painted a picture of people living in three earthly generations who know each other and interact in heaven. Since Abraham is now enjoying the company of his son and grandson, the term "gathered to his people" obviously has a meaning beyond the grave. Based on these scriptures, it is reasonable and logical to believe that in heaven, we, too, will experience continuity of relationships.

We find another biblical example of continuity in the account of the transfiguration of Christ (Luke 9:28–35). Jesus ascended a mountain, and at the top He temporarily transfigured into His glorious heavenly appearance. Moses and Elijah appeared with

Him, and both of these long-departed men were recognized and named by Peter, James, and John. This incident shows us three things about continuity: first, that in heaven, Moses and Elijah are still who they were on earth. They even retained their earthly names. Second, in heaven people continue their earthly, God-given vocations—in the case of Moses and Elijah, their roles as prophets and leaders of God's people. Third, the transfiguration shows that humans on earth can recognize citizens of heaven.

The scriptures we have studied in this section show us that in heaven we continue to be who we are on earth. Continuity of our personalities, our appearances, and our manners of expression will allow us to recognize each other. Continuity of our talents and abilities will allow us to continue the kind of work we enjoyed on earth.

Aside from Scripture, what do some of our prominent authors and theologians tell us about continuity? In *The Divine Conspiracy*, Dallas Willard affirmed his belief in the continuity of life: "The life we now have as the persons we now are will continue, and continue in the universe in which we now exist."[7]

Randy Alcorn put it this way:

When we get in the car, we turn on our favorite music and head home to barbecue with friends, watch a ball game, play golf, ride bikes, work in the garden, or curl up with a cup of coffee and a good book. We do these things not because we are sinners but because we are people. We will still be people when we die and go to Heaven. This isn't a disappointing reality—it's God's plan. He made us as we are—except the sin part, which has nothing to do with friends, eating, sports, gardening, or reading.[8]

Here is a natural follow-up question: "When we are in heaven, will we remember the past?" The answer: "Of course!" Without memory, we are nothing. In heaven we will know the past as we live our eternal future.

In his book *Exploring Heaven*, Arthur O. Roberts said, "Death is not the last word. Life is the final word and that life includes conscious personal continuation beyond the tunnel of death."[9] He then offered this perspective on the continuity of memory: "In heaven all memories, good and bad will be woven into one's personal redemptive story, like a prelude to a fuller story of life with God in company with redeemed humanity, in a recreated cosmos."[10]

So for now we await the joys of heaven, but let us not forget that our work on earth will never be wasted. N. T. Wright put it this way: "When the final resurrection occurs, as the centerpiece of God's new creation, we will discover that everything done in the present world in the power of Jesus's own resurrection will be celebrated and included, appropriately transformed.'"[11]

We can see that continuity of our lives and personhood from earth to heaven is a biblically sound doctrine. And the transition may turn out to be more seamless than we can imagine. In his book *Soul Keeping*, John Ortberg quoted a line from a personal conversation he had with Dallas Willard about dying. Willard said, "I think that when I die, it may take some time before I know it."[12]

The truth of the continuity from earth to heaven is a cause for celebration! Someday I will be reunited with Harriet. I will know her, and she will know me. Although I now miss her every second of every day, the knowledge that our separation is temporary gives me energy for my mission on earth and great expectations for the future.

THE COMMUNITY OF HEAVENLY CITIZENS

On earth, citizenship in a stable nation is both a privilege and a responsibility. The Bible confirms that our citizenship in heaven also includes both of these aspects of life in community. The following verses confirm that we have been granted heavenly citizenship even though at present we live on earth:

You are fellow citizens with the saints. (Ephesians 2:19)

For our citizenship is in heaven, from which also we eagerly wait for a Savior, the Lord Jesus Christ. (Philippians 3:20)

Why is it so important to understand the community aspect of heaven? An incident in the book of Acts involving Paul and his missionary companion, Silas, illustrates the answer. Their preaching in the Roman city of Philippi caused a riot, and as a result, Roman soldiers arrested the two men, beat them, and threw them into prison overnight. In the morning, the magistrates sent word to the jailer to release them. Here is Paul's response to the messenger:

"They have beaten us in public without trial, men who are Romans, and have thrown us into prison; and now are they sending us away secretly? No indeed! But let them come themselves and bring us out." The policemen reported these words to the chief magistrates. They were afraid when they heard that they were Romans. (Acts 16:37–38)

The Philippian officials had cause to be afraid. Roman citizens had significant protections, privileges, and civil rights that non-Romans lacked, and there were severe penalties for violating those rights.

Like Rome, all kingdoms certify citizens and grant them certain rights and privileges. We know from Scripture that heaven is a kingdom. We acknowledge this fact every time we recite the words "Your kingdom come" in the Lord's Prayer (Matthew 6:10). The kingdom nature of heaven is also indicated by the fact that it has cities. We see this fact in Jesus' parable of the talents when the master rewards his servant, saying, "Well done, good slave, because you have been faithful in a very little thing, you are to be in authority over ten cities" (Luke 19:17).

Heaven is also called a country. "But as it is, they desire a better country, that is, a heavenly one. Therefore God is not ashamed to be called their God; for He has prepared a city for them" (Hebrews 11:16).

From all three of these perspectives (kingdom, country, and city), we can see that heaven is a place for people to live. It is a community of citizens who belong to God's kingdom and have all the privileges, joys, fellowship, and responsibilities appropriate to it. In heaven we will serve a King who directs our service as His citizens. So citizenship in heaven means delightful, satisfying tasks linked to the unique skills and talents He has given each of us.

It is a place where we will delight in the warmth of community. People are by nature social creatures. We enjoy interacting with others. Can you imagine getting to know people of every tribe and tongue and nation? Heaven is a melting pot of nationalities that will never view each other with suspicion, superiority, or hostility; they will blend socially into a harmonious whole. We can see the joy of this blending in these beautiful words from Revelation:

And they sang a new song, saying,

"Worthy are You to take the book and to break its seals; for You were slain, and purchased for God with Your blood men from every tribe and tongue and people and nation." (5:9)

One day all believers from all the nations on earth will be citizens of one country—heaven. Yet we will retain our uniqueness while embracing the uniqueness of others. If you are Ethiopian, you will always be Ethiopian. Why would you be different? I am looking forward to meeting the remarkable Ethiopian eunuch whom Philip led to Christ in Acts 8:26–36. Or maybe Simon from Cyrene, who bore the cross of Jesus. Or maybe one of the wise men, possibly Asians, who followed the star to Jesus from the East.

Harriet loved people. She never met a stranger. I can imagine the joy she is having in meeting new people who are her fellow citizens of heaven. And I know she greets those she knew on earth when they enter heaven.

One of my last and most precious memories of Harriet's people-loving spirit was forever imprinted in my mind and heart at the Atlanta airport. We had arrived early for our flight home after enjoying a visit with our grandkids. Harriet suddenly remembered she had left her back pillow in the rental car. I stood up to retrieve it just as a handsome, well-dressed black man the size of an NFL linebacker sat down across from us in one of the four chairs in the waiting area. He looked visibly upset, and Harriet immediately introduced herself and asked the gentleman if he was okay.

He sighed deeply and said, "No, I'm not okay. I just lost a major vendor contract with the airport." He went on to explain that he was the sole supporter of his family, and he was trying to get his kids into good schools. It was a crushing financial setback for him.

Realizing the essence of time, I explained that I had to dash to the car lot to retrieve Harriet's pillow. As I departed, she and the man continued their conversation. When I returned fifteen minutes later, this huge man was sitting on the sidearm of Harriet's chair. She was holding his hand, sharing Christ with him, and praying for his situation.

I stood back and watched in awe as my petite wife ministered to this huge man with a Goliath-size need. It was a picture of Christlike love that I will never forget. Knowing Harriet, I'm sure that she continues to pray for this man, his business, and his family from her new home in heaven. And when he enters heaven someday, I know he will seek her out. She will forever be a part of his family.

The Delight of Worshiping God

As citizens of heaven, our highest delight, honor, and privilege will be our worship of God. He seeks our worship, not only because He deserves it but also because it draws us into His joy and glory. This means that in heaven, worship is thrilling!

Worship is another element in which we see continuity from earth to heaven. God desires in heaven people who worshiped Him on earth. Jesus said, "But an hour is coming, and now is, when the true worshipers will worship the Father in spirit and truth; for such people the Father seeks to be His worshipers" (John 4:23).

The book of Revelation opens the curtain on several scenes that reveal the worship we will enjoy in heaven. These scenes are so grand, expansive, massive, and thrilling that I need do little more in this chapter than let these eloquent pictures speak for themselves.

First, we will feel free to shout out loud our love for Christ and our awe of what He has done for us:

> Then I looked, and I heard the voice of many angels around the throne and the living creatures and the elders; and the number of them was myriads of myriads, and thousands of thousands, saying with a *loud voice*,
> "Worthy is the Lamb that was slain to receive power and riches and wisdom and might and honor and glory and blessing."
> (Revelation 5:11–12)

Not only humans, but every living creature will join in the glorious praise in heaven:

> And every created thing which is in heaven and on the earth and under the earth and on the sea, and all things in them, I heard saying,
> "To Him who sits on the throne, and to the Lamb, be blessing and honor and glory and dominion forever and ever."
> And the four living creatures kept saying, "Amen." And the elders fell down and worshiped. (Revelation 5:13–14)

Next we see what may well be the largest worship service ever held in this universe:

> After these things I looked, and behold, a great multitude which no one could count, from every nation and all tribes and peoples and tongues, standing before the throne and before the Lamb, clothed in white robes, and palm branches were in their hands; and they *cry out with a loud voice, saying,*

"Salvation to our God who sits on the throne, and to the Lamb."
(Revelation 7:9–10)

We will have the thrilling privilege of worshiping side by side with angels:

And all the angels were standing around the throne and around the elders and the four living creatures; and they fell on their faces before the throne and worshiped God, saying,

"Amen, blessings and glory and wisdom and thanksgiving and honor and power and might, be to our God forever and ever. Amen." (Revelation 7:11–12)

Notice in these next verses that in heaven, the worshiping multitudes sing songs written on earth—in this instance the song of Moses. I have no reason to doubt that we will sing with others our favorite hymns there.

And I saw something like a sea of glass mixed with fire, and those who had been victorious over the beast and his image and the number of his name, standing on the sea of glass, holding harps of God. And they *sang the song of Moses*, the bond-servant of God, and the song of the Lamb, saying,

"Great and marvelous are Your works,
O Lord God, the Almighty;
Righteous and true are Your ways,
King of the nations!
Who will not fear, O Lord, and glorify Your name?
For You alone are holy;

For all the nations will come and worship before You,
For Your righteous acts have been revealed." (Revelation
15:2–4)

I imagine Harriet worshiping God in heaven, mightily singing her favorite hymns, her heart bursting with joy, her mind filled with absolute delight at the sight of myriad worshipers, and her ears tuned to the choruses of angels singing praise to God. It thrills my heart to imagine her freedom of expression. And I anticipate with the greatest of joy the day that I, too, will be able to love and worship God in heaven with all my heart, soul, mind, and strength.

From all that we have learned about heaven and the glories that await us there, isn't it amazing that God has even provided a welcome party, and all our loved ones can't wait for us to arrive? I can see Harriet's excitement when I walk through those gates, and I anticipate her open arms stretched forward, eager to hold me tighter than ever before. And then I can see her turning and pointing toward Jesus, and for the first time I see face-to-face the true lover of my soul, who will hold me in His love forever.

It's Not the Gift;
It's the Giver

While writing *Visits from Heaven*, I realized how much God's gift of the dreams of Harriet have helped me to find a new perspective on my priorities. During those first weeks after her death, as I was being tossed mercilessly on great waves of grief, it would have been easy to reach out and cling to those dreams as my life raft. But over the years, I have come to see that the dreams God has given me are not an end within themselves. They are pointers designed to refocus my vision on a higher reality.

I don't need dreams; I need God. He is ultimately my only source of comfort. Yes, the dreams are gifts from Him, but their intent is to get me to depend not on the gifts but on the Giver. He wants me to find comfort not in the dreams but in the source of them.

When describing Moses parting the Red Sea, the Bible does not focus on *how* God did it but on *why* He did it. God wanted to show Moses and the children of Israel how mightily He would care for them and protect them.

Recognizing this truth, I often return to the apostle Paul's words to the Colossians:

Therefore if you have been raised up with Christ, *keep seeking* the things above, where Christ is, seated at the right hand of

God. *Set your mind* on the things above, not on the things that are on earth. (3:1–2)

Twice Paul encouraged believers to focus on "the things above." He repeated the phrase for emphasis. Why is this command so crucial? Because "the things above" are where reality resides. Heaven is our destination, our future. Learning about heaven and our life there should become our quest. The burdens and griefs of earth will become bearable when we set our minds on "the things above" and realize these truths about heaven:

- Heaven is a real place—and it is where God resides.

Pray, then, in this way:

> "Our Father who is in heaven,
> Hallowed be Your name." (Matthew 6:9)

- Life on earth is a test, and it has a limit.

Each man's work will become evident; for the day will show it because it is to be revealed with fire, and the fire itself will test the quality of each man's work. (1 Corinthians 3:13)

- We can store up treasure and reward in heaven.

But store up for yourselves treasures in heaven, where neither moth nor rust destroys, and where thieves do not break in or steal; for where your treasure is, there your heart will be also. (Matthew 6:20–21)

- This journey will be examined because it is valuable to God and to you.

For the Son of Man is going to come in the glory of His Father with His angels, and will then repay every man according to his deeds. (Matthew 16:27)

If you address as Father the One who impartially judges according to each one's work, conduct yourselves in fear during the time of your stay on earth. (1 Peter 1:17)

- By setting your mind on heaven, you are expressing faith, and faith pleases God. He is our highest desire.

And without faith it is impossible to please Him, for he who comes to God must believe that He is and that He is a rewarder of those who seek Him. (Hebrews 11:6)

Setting our minds on heaven does not, as some have claimed, render us too other-focused to be useful citizens in this world. In fact, the opposite is true. In Jesus' parable of the talents (Matthew 25:14–30), those servants who were most dedicated to their master (who represents God) were the ones who accomplished the most on earth. And their earthly accomplishments earned his reward. A well-known quote by C. S. Lewis from *Mere Christianity* expresses the point perfectly: "If you read history you will find that the Christians who did most for the present world were just those who thought most of the next."[1]

Now, several years after Harriet's death, heaven's joys have become so much clearer to me. I look forward to seeing her again one day, but for now, I am warmed by these truths:

1. She is in God's hands.
2. She is happy and at peace.
3. She has purpose in living for Him.
4. She has responsibilities.
5. She is focused, not aimless.
6. She is learning more about the wisdom of God.
7. She is using her God-given gifts.
8. She is seeing her whole life in light of God's plan.
9. She is reuniting with her family members.
10. She is meeting members of my family.
11. She is worshiping with the greatest joy ever.
12. She is praying for God's plan on earth.
13. She has a godly grief for me.
14. She prays for me and with me and her family on earth.
15. She experiences the grace of God every day, just as I do.
16. She sees Jesus face-to-face.

As I imagine Harriet living her abundant new life, I am more in love with her than ever. I can't wait for her to teach me the expanding mysteries that she is experiencing and to learn through my own experience how much more real Christ is to those who see Him face-to-face! What a visit that will be!

ACKNOWLEDGMENTS

I owe a huge debt of gratitude to Randy Alcorn. C. S. Lewis once said that George MacDonald baptized his imagination. MacDonald used fantasy to teach biblical truth, and Lewis credits him with releasing his imagination. This is what Randy has done for me. His work on heaven and his novels that expand on the logical possibilities of heaven gave me a new freedom to develop what I call the *lens of logic*. And one more credit is his *Eternal Perspectives*, a 658-page volume of quotes that he gained from his research. I have used many of them and have also gone back to their original sources to learn even more.

I also want to thank Vickey Gardner, Corey Page, and Nancy Ross for the many editions they typed. Nancy chased sources for me continually. My new best friend is Ivey Beckman. She polished and repolished my words and made me sound a lot better than I really am.

I want to thank Park Cities Presbyterian Church. Its staff and leadership helped me through my darkest days, encouraged me to tell my story, and gave me time to research it. Its members and my best friends prayed me through the hard days, so much that I felt the eagle's wings mounting up underneath me. Specifically, the

Covenant Class listened to my series on heaven and encouraged me to write.

And a big thank you to Kathy Peel, who encouraged me to write this book and got me started on the pathway to publishing.

I also want to thank Robert Wolgemuth and Austin Wilson of Wolgemuth and Associates for believing in the book.

Finally, I want to thank the wonderful team from W Publishing Group. Debbie Wickwire continued to inspire me with her excitement about this book. Tom Williams and Jennifer Stair gave it tremendous improvements, polish, and cohesion. Their whole team is amazing.

What a joy to "commune" as saints together on this project! May God be glorified.

Notes

Chapter 3: An Earth-Shattering Instant

1. Ron Rolheiser, "Losing a Loved One to Suicide," June 7, 1998, http://ronrolheiser.com/losing-a-loved-one-to-suicide/#.VtZ0XdAk_ww.

Chapter 4: Heaven's Compassion

1. Eleanor H. Hull, "Be Thou My Vision," public domain.
2. John Claypool, *Tracks of a Fellow Struggler* (Harrisburg, PA: Morehouse, 2004).
3. John Claypool, *The Hopeful Heart* (New York: Church Publishing, 2003); John Claypool, *Mending the Heart* (Cambridge, MA: Cowley, 1999); John Claypool, *God Is an Amateur* (Cincinnati: Forward Movement, 1994).
4. Claypool, *God Is an Amateur*, 59.
5. Claypool, *The Hopeful Heart*, 77.
6. Henry Drummond, *The Greatest Thing in the World and Other Addresses*, Greetings Books series (New York: Collins, 1970).
7. Sheldon Vanauken, *A Severe Mercy* (New York: Harper and Row, 1977), 188.
8. Claypool, *God Is an Amateur*, 38.

Chapter 5: When the Dream Gate Opened

1. Henry Edward Manning, "Sermon XVIII: The Communion of Saints," *Sermons*, vol. 4 (London: William Pickering, 1850; repr. Grand Rapids: Christian Classics Ethereal Library, n.d.), 145–46.
2. F. Scott Fitzgerald, *The Great Gatsby* (New York: Scribner, 2004), 48; emphasis in original.
3. C. S. Lewis, *The Business of Heaven* (Mariner, 1984); Billy Graham, *The Heaven Answer Book* (Nashville: Thomas Nelson, 2012); Joni Eareckson Tada, *Heaven* (Grand Rapids: Zondervan, 1997); Paul Enns, *Heaven*

Revealed (Chicago: Moody, 2011); and Randy Alcorn, *Heaven* (Carol Stream, IL: Tyndale, 2004).

4. C. S. Lewis, *A Grief Observed* (New York: HarperOne, 2015), 70–71.

5. Sheldon Vanauken, *A Severe Mercy* (New York: HarperOne, 2009), 221–23; emphasis in original.

6. Ibid., 221, 223.

7. Dallas Willard, quoted in Bob P. Buford, *Finishing Well* (Nashville: Integrity, 2004), 18.

Chapter 6: Questions for Heaven

1. J. I. Packer, *Guard Us, Guide Us* (Grand Rapids: Baker, 2008), 208–10.

2. Ibid., 199–200; emphasis added.

3. Dallas Willard, *Hearing God* (Downers Grove, IL: InterVarsity, 2012), 115.

4. Morton T. Kelsey, *Dreams* (Mahwah, NJ: Paulist, 1978), 72–74.

5. Eric Metaxas, "The Golden Fish: How God Woke Me Up in a Dream," *Christianity Today* 57, no. 5 (June 2013), http://www.christianitytoday.com/ct/2013/june/golden-fish-eric-metaxas.html; emphasis in original.

Chapter 7: Gifts of Grace—More Dreams

1. Richard Rohr, *Everything Belongs: The Gift of Contemplative Prayer* (New York, Crossroad, 2003), 135.

2. Bill Watterson, *Calvin and Hobbes*, January 13, 1991, http://www.gocomics.com/calvinandhobbes/1991/01/13.

3. George MacDonald, *Lilith* (1895; repr. Grand Rapids: Eerdman's, 2000), 251.

Chapter 8: The Landscape of Grief

1. John Claypool, *Tracks of a Fellow Struggler* (Harrisburg, PA: Morehouse, 2004), 12.

2. John Claypool, *Mending the Heart* (Cambridge, MA: Cowley, 1999), 57.

3. James Means, *A Tearful Celebration* (Colorado Springs: Multnomah, 2006), 46.

4. Jerry L. Sittser, *A Grace Disguised* (Grand Rapids: Zondervan, 2009), 45; emphasis in original.

5. Dietrich Bonhoeffer, *God Is in the Manger* (Louisville, KY: Westminster John Knox, 2010), 4.

6. Michael O'Brien, *Sophia House* (San Francisco: Ignatius, 2005; repr. 2006), 171.

7. Sittser, *A Grace Disguised*, 160.

Chapter 9: How Death Changed the Way I Live

1. David Ray, "Thanks, Robert Frost," *Music of Time: Selected and New Poems* (Omaha, NE: Backwaters, 2006).
2. Francis Schaeffer, *Art and the Bible* (Downers Grove, IL: InterVarsity, 1973), 61.
3. Randy Alcorn, ed., *We Shall See God* (Carol Stream, IL: Tyndale, 2011), 86.
4. *Man of Steel*, directed by Zack Snyder (Burbank, CA: Warner Home Video, 2013), DVD.

Chapter 10: Climbing the Ladder of Truth

1. Wayne Grudem, *Systematic Theology* (Grand Rapids: Zondervan, 1994), 197.
2. John Claypool, "The Worst Things Are Never the Last Things," from the Chicago Sunday Evening Club's *30 Good Minutes*, program 3218, February 5, 1989, http://www.30goodminutes.org/index.php/support -us/23-member-archives/711-john-claypool-program-3218.
3. James Means, *A Tearful Celebration* (Colorado Springs: Multnomah, 2006), 38.
4. John Claypool, *Tracks of a Fellow Struggler* (Harrisburg, PA: Morehouse, 2004), 65–66.
5. Ibid., 66.

Chapter 11: Amazing Heaven—Its Setting

1. Randy Alcorn, *Heaven* (Carol Stream, IL: Tyndale, 2004).
2. John Gilmore, *Probing Heaven* (Grand Rapids: Baker, 1989); Arthur O. Roberts, *Exploring Heaven* (San Francisco: HarperSanFrancisco, 2003); Peter Kreeft, *Everything You Ever Wanted to Know About Heaven* (San Francisco: Ignatius, 1990).
3. Gilmore, *Probing Heaven*, 91–92.
4. Randy Alcorn, ed., *We Shall See God* (Carol Stream, IL: Tyndale, 2011), 124.
5. Brooke Foss Wescott, *The Epistle to the Hebrews* (Grand Rapids: Zondervan, 2007), EPUB download, chap. 11, 1663, https://archive.org /details/epistletohebrew00westgoog.
6. J. Sidlow Baxter, *The Other Side of Death* (Grand Rapids: Kregel, 1997), 61; italics in original.
7. N. T. Wright, *Surprised by Hope* (New York: HarperOne, 2008), 170.
8. Ibid.
9. Nicolas Berdyaev, *The Divine and the Human* (San Rafael, CA: Semantron, 2009), 139.
10. Jonathan Edwards, quoted in John Gerstner, *Jonathan Edwards on Heaven and Hell* (Grand Rapids: Baker, 1980), 24.

CHAPTER 12: AMAZING HEAVEN—ITS PEOPLE

1. Charles Spurgeon, "The First Resurrection," sermon #391, Metropolitan Tabernacle, Newington, May 5, 1861.

2. Arthur O. Roberts, *Exploring Heaven* (San Francisco: HarperSanFrancisco, 2003), 110.

3. Steven J. Lawson, *Heaven Help Us!* (Colorado Springs: NavPress, 1995), 194.

4. Edward Donnelly, *Biblical Teaching on the Doctrines of Heaven and Hell* (Edinburgh: Banner of Truth, 2001), 123.

5. Dallas Willard, as quoted in John Ortberg, *Soul Keeping* (Grand Rapids: Zondervan, 2014), 22.

6. William Hendricksen, *The Bible on the Life Hereafter* (Grand Rapids: Baker, 1959), 75–76; italics in original.

7. Dallas Willard, *The Divine Conspiracy* (New York: HarperCollins, 1998), 395.

8. Randy Alcorn, *50 Days of Heaven* (Carol Stream, IL: Tyndale, 2006), 115.

9. Roberts, *Exploring Heaven*, 33.

10. Ibid., 111.

11. N. T. Wright, *Surprised by Hope* (New York: HarperCollins, 2008), 294.

12. Dallas Willard, as quoted in John Ortberg, *Soul Keeping* (Grand Rapids: Zondervan, 2014), 162.

IT'S NOT THE GIFT; IT'S THE GIVER

1. C. S. Lewis, *Mere Christianity* (New York: HarperOne, 2015), 132.

ABOUT THE AUTHOR

DR. PETE DEISON is a pastor, teacher, and president of Park Cities Presbyterian Church Foundation. He has served as a pastor in the Presbyterian Church of America since 1978 and was on the national team directing the campus ministry of CRU. He now serves as associate pastor of Park Cities Presbyterian Church in Dallas, Texas, where he has directed the men's ministry, workplace ministries, evangelism, and officer training, and where he currently teaches a large adult Sunday school class. He is a featured speaker at the Kanakuk Institute and the author of *The Priority of Knowing God*. Pete has two married daughters and eight awesome grandchildren, is an avid fisherman, and loves to travel.